The History of Elmira, New York

by Hon. Thomas Maxwell, 1863

and the Elmira City Directory 1863

Restored by New York History Review

The History of Elmira, New York and the Elmira City Directory 1863
by Hon. Thomas Maxwell and New York History Review
Copyright ©2022 New York History Review. Some rights reserved.

Notice of Rights. No part of this book may be reproduced or transmitted in any form by any means, mechanical, photocopying, recording or otherwise, without the prior written permission of the author. For more information on getting permission for reprints contact us through our website. NewYorkHistoryReview.com

ISBN: 978-1-950822-29-4

Printed in the United States of America.

Elmira's railroad depot on Wisner Street, now Railroad Avenue, circa 1855.

PREFACE.

DIRECTORY making in Elmira has usually been unprofitable business, both for the publisher and patrons of the book. We tried it as an experiment under circumstances somewhat discouraging, and, thanks to the liberality of the business men, it has proven a complete success. We have endeavored to make a book worthy of your praise, and now invite the criticisms of our patrons; but for the opinions of non-paying fault-finders and professional grumblers we care nothing.

For the History of Elmira by Hon. THOMAS MAXWELL, we need not bespeak a careful perusal, as the name of the author who has passed the "three score years and ten" among the scenes of Chemung Valley and now enjoys the vigor of youth, is sufficient to give it universal popularity.

Especial attention is directed to the advertisements of the Seneca Lake Steamers on pages IV and 58. This is a speedy, safe and pleasant route—both steamers being commanded by unexceptionable gentlemen.

We here take occasion to call attention to William Brown's hardware card on the outside of the front cover.

For the superior manner in which the typography of the work is executed, we are indebted to the mechanical skill employed by FAIRMAN & DE VOE in their job printing office, and the binding is the work of Mr. LOUIS KIES, who is connected with their establishment.

To the Editorial Fraternity we are indebted for many favors shown us, and shall hail with joy the opportunity to reciprocate.

To all who have assisted us—THANK YOU.

THE PUBLISHER.

ELMIRA, February, 1863.

SENECA LAKE.

Shortest, Quickest, Cheapest and Best Route
FOR
ALBANY, TROY, UTICA, SYRACUSE, AUBURN, WATERLOO, SENECA FALLS & GENEVA.

ALSO, FROM THE NORTH FOR

Elmira, Williamsport, Philadelphia, Harrisburg, Baltimore, Washington, and all points on the Erie, and Williamsport & Elmira Railways.

THROUGH IN 24 HOURS

FROM GENEVA TO WASHINGTON, WITHOUT DETENTION.

THE SPLENDID LOW-PRESSURE STEAMER

D. S. MAGEE,
(CAPT. D. P. DEY,)

Will leave WATKINS at 3.30 P. M., on arrival of train from the South, arriving at GENEVA in time to connect with the evening train for ALBANY, BUFFALO, and all points East and West on the NEW YORK CENTRAL RAILROAD.

RETURNING,

Will leave GENEVA at 8.30 A. M., arriving at WATKINS in time for the train South, which connects at ELMIRA with trains for all points East and South on the ERIE RAILWAY and ELMIRA & WILLIAMSPORT R. R.

☞ The Steamer D. S. MAGEE connects at DRESDEN, morning and evening, with Stage for PENN YAN.

INDEX TO ADVERTISEMENTS.

Arnot S T, Seneca Lake steamers,...... 58
Ayres S, watches, jewelry & ins,...... 156
Baldwin & Reynolds, mer tailors,...... 116
Bartholomew U, tobacconist,............ 96
Brown Wm, hardware,...outside ft. cover
Burns Thomas, grocer,...................... 108
Coke Levi, baker & confectioner,...... 166
Cass John, mer tailor,........................ 160
Collingwood Bro, watches & jewelry, 116
Comstock S G, hats, caps, &c,.......... 80
Cook & Covell, hardware,................. 60
Covell E & Co, dry goods,................ 114
Covell John D, druggist,.................... 118
Cowen & Son, auction & commission, 168
Derby A L, boots & shoes,................ 88
Dey D P, Seneca Lake steamers........ IV
Dexter & Elmore, crockery &c,........ 84
Eliason, Greener & Co, piano manufs, 86
Elmira Advertiser, S. B. Fairman..... 5
Elmira Gazette, F A DeVoe............. VIII
Elmira Press, Thayer & Whitley,..... 6
Elmira Water Cure, S O Gleason,.... 100
Fairman & DeVoe, job printers,...... VII
Gardiner N W, hats, caps &c,.......... 72
Gill Brothers, tobacconists,............... 110
Gridley & Davenport, hardware,...... 150
Hall Brothers, booksellers, &c,......... 8
Halliday Wm, Elmira steam mills.... 62
Hamilton Charles, saloon,................. 142
Hart A P, photographer, outside front cover..
Hart Wm E, dry goods,...................... 94
Haskell W H, dry goods,................... 126
Hotchkin Samuel, Elmira mills........ 158
Hubbell S B, furniture,...................... 70
Hutchinson S S, boots & shoes,........ 72

Jones Joshua, Arbour Hotel,............ 74
Kies Louis, book binder,................... VI
Lehman E & Co, mer tailors, &c,..... 66
Levy Maurice, tobacconist,............... 110
Lormore W J, grocer,....................... 64
McCarty Michael, marble dealer,..... 142
McGreevy Owen, livery,................... 124
McIntire H W, shingle machine,..... 110
Marsh Wash, painter,........................ 98
Merwin W, harness &c,.................... 88
Morris R, grocer,................................ 108
Nicks John I, tobacconist,................. 90
Northrup O B, boots & shoes,........... 122
Pattinson T S, meat market,............. 64
Perry & Scott, insurance agents,..... 154
Perry John K, druggist,.................... 160
Post G H, union coffee mills,............ 82
Potter C T, livery,............................. 4
Preswick & Dudley, booksellers &c,. 7
Rathbun's Brainard House, C Slater, outside back cover..............................
Rice, Durland & Pratt, dry goods,.... 78
Richardson M, dry goods,................. 92
Scardefield G W & Co, gilders and frame manufacturers,..................... 74
Smith E B, baker & confectioner,..... 118
Smith Harvey, groceries,.................. 96
Stuart & Ufford, mer tailors,............ 138
Tillman J M, harness &c,.................. 110
Tuthill, Brooks & Co, dry goods,...... 68
Up DeGraff Thad S, occulist & aurist, 102
Waters G W, portrait painter,.......... 142
Watrous R, hardware,....................... 106
West C F, Arnot's mills,................... 167
Williams E, grocer,............................ 76
Yates Wm P, watches & jewelry,..... 86

BOOK BINDERY,

LAKE STREET, ELMIRA.

FAIRMAN & CO., Proprietors.

This old established Bindery, having been recently fitted up with a variety of Apparatus and Tools of the newest styles, and being constantly supplied with a choice selection of

SUPERIOR BINDERS' STOCK,

we feel confident of pleasing all in every variety of work needed by our customers.

BLANK BOOKS,

Including the heaviest full bound LEDGERS and RECORD BOOKS, with or without Printed Headings, JOURNALS, DAY BOOKS, and every kind and style of Blank Books made to order.

Paper Ruled to any desired Pattern,

LETTERING, STAMPING & GILDING done nicely to order.

All ordinary Binding and Ruling done as usual, and ALL WORK WARRANTED.

S. B. FAIRMAN,
F. A. DE VOE,
LOUIS KIES.
} FAIRMAN & CO.

ELMIRA
STEAM PRINTING HOUSE
LAKE STREET, ELMIRA, N. Y.

FAIRMAN & DE VOE,
PROPRIETORS.

THE ample and varied stock of Type material, the Four Power Presses driven by Steam, and the experience of the skillful workmen employed in the above establishment, enable the proprietors to promise to the public the prompt execution of all orders for every variety of

Plain and Ornamental Book and Job Printing,
in the best manner and on the most reasonable terms.

Particular attention is invited to their facilities for doing all kinds of Ruled Blank Work, Legal Printing and Book and Pamphlet Work.

Orders from a distance respectfully solicited and promptly filled.

S. B. FAIRMAN.   F. A. DE VOE.

Elmira Daily Gazette,

ISSUED EVERY EVENING,

(SUNDAYS EXCEPTED,)

At the Corner of Lake and Water streets, Elmira, N. Y.

F. A. DE VOE, PROPRIETOR.

It is delivered to Village Subscribers, by the Carrier, at $5.00 per annum, payable quarterly, or ten cents per week, payable to the Carrier; and is mailed to subscribers out of the village at $4.00 per annum, payable in advance.

Elmira Weekly Gazette,

ISSUED EVERY THURSDAY MORNING,

CORNER OF LAKE AND WATER STREETS,

ELMIRA, N. Y.

F. A. DE VOE, PROPRIETOR.

It is mailed to any part of the country, or delivered at the office, to regular subscribers, at $1.50 per annum, payable in advance; if not paid in advance, $2.00 per annum. Village subscribers, served by the Carrier, $2.00 per annum, payable in advance; if not paid in advance, $2.50.

ELMIRA.

AS A HISTORY OF THE BUSINESS OF ELMIRA, we present the following notices of some of our advertisers.

MESSRS. E. COVELL & Co., dealers in dry goods and groceries, at No. 106 Water street, are the proprietors of a business established in 1807 by TUTHILL & COVELL, who continued it until 1830, when Mr. T. retired from the firm and the junior member, Mr. Robert Covell, Senior, continued the business. In 1834 Mr. Robert Covell, Junior, became a partner in the house, and in 1839 Mr. Edward Covell took the interest of R. Covell, Senior, and since that time, with the exception of three years, the business has been conducted by the Messrs. E. & R. Covell. They have a store 25 by 66, at all times filled with a complete stock of goods for the accommodation of their large trade. See card, page 114.

TUTHILL, BROOKS & Co., dealers in dry goods, &c., at No. 132 (old No. 34) Water street. This house was established in 1831, by the senior member of the present firm, Mr. David H. Tuthill, who has ever since that time been connected with the business, except during an interval of two years. They have a store 25 by 90, four stories high, and unite with their large experience in the dry goods trade, well known ability, which with their manner of dealing, gives them a large trade. See card, page 68.

The Dry Goods House of Messrs. RICE, DURLAND & PRATT, at No. 122 Water street, was established in 1840, by S. S. & J. Hamlin, and in 1861 the present firm was formed, Mr. Rice, the senior member, having been connected with the house since 1846. They have a store 20 by 106, well filled with staple and fancy dry goods and carpets, and for the advantage of their large list of patrons, combine experience and ability in the conduct of their trade. See card, page 78.

WILLIAM E. HART, dealer in dry goods, groceries &c., at No. 110

Water street, commenced his business here in 1842, and has been in trade uninterruptedly since that time. He has a store 22 by 85, and always has a complete assortment of goods in his line. During his twenty years experience here, Mr. Hart has gained a large business and many friends as a reward for his attention to the wants of his patrons. See card, page 94.

A very popular dry goods house is to be found at No. 107 Water street, (6 Union Block,) and an equally popular proprietor in the person of Mr. M. RICHARDSON, who commenced trade in Elmira in 1859. He has a store 22 by 80, the full capacity of which is taxed to accommodate his patrons, who here find every thing in the line of Dry Goods, and are always pleased. See card, page 92.

WILLIAM H. HASKELL, at No 7 Baldwin street, commenced the dry goods trade here in the Fall of 1862, and has already fully convinced the people of his ability to supply their wants at fair prices. At his store can be found a full assortment, and the best comment on his manner of dealing is the extent of his trade and the universal satisfaction which he gives his patrons. See card, page 126.

An immense house is that of STUART & UFFORD, merchant tailors, &c., at No. 20 and 22 Lake street. In 1854 Mr. Charles B. Stuart commenced trade here. In 1857 the firm of William Beach & Co. was formed, of which Mr. Daniel E. Ufford was a member, and in 1859 the houses of C. B. Stuart and William Beach & Co. were united, and the firm became Beach, Stuart & Co. In 1860 Mr. B. retired from the house and the proprietorship passed into the hands of Stuart & Ufford. They occupy two stores, each 20 by 100, ground floor and basement, filled with an almost endless variety of clothing, boots and shoes, hats and caps, furs, military goods, trunks, &c., &c., and their extensive trade demands all their facilities, requiring them to keep a large force constantly employed manufacturing all kinds of goods for the sales-room, and to the manufacturing of goods to order, they give very particular attention. See card, page 138.

BALDWIN & REYNOLDS, merchant tailors, &c., at No. 149 Water street commenced trade here in 1858, and have, by giving their patrons the benefit of long experience and close attention to business gained a large and valuable trade. Their store is 24 by 70, well filled with clothing, furnishing goods, &c. To the merchant tailoring department of their business, is given particular attention, and in this branch they excel. See card, page 116.

The Merchant Tailoring and Clothing House of E. LEHMAN & Co., at No. 151 Water street was opened in the Spring of 1861, and since that time has become a popular resort for buyers who wish to get the full value of their investment. The merchant tailoring department is under the personal supervision of Mr. Lehman, the senior member of the firm, a gentleman of much skill and experience as exhibited daily in his business. Their store is 20 by 60, and is all needed for their extensive trade. See card, page 66.

JOHN CASS, merchant tailor and clothier, on the corner of Water and Baldwin streets, has been in trade in Elmira during the last fourteen years, and in the Fall of 1861 commenced his present business, having been in the dry goods trade previous to that time. He has a store 24 by 90, and the immense trade which he enjoys fully attests his popularity as a dealer. See card, page 160.

N. W. GARDINER, dealer in Hats, Caps, Furs, &c., at No. 117, Water street, opened his trade here in 1837, in a store occupying the same lot where he now is, and has from time to time, as the increase of his business demanded, enlarged his facilities. His store is 20 by 50 and well filled with good goods and he enjoys an extensive business. See card, page 72.

In the Spring of 1855, S. G. COMSTOCK commenced his trade in hats, caps, furs, &c., at No. 150 Water street, and now enjoys as a just result of his liberality of dealing and universal custom of pleasing his patrons, a lucrative first class trade. His store is 22 by 50, and its utmost capacity is taxed for the conducting of his business, which is continually increasing. See card, page 80.

The oldest hardware dealer in Elmira is R. WATROUS at No. 112 Water Street. Mr. W. commenced trade in this village in 1838, as a member of the firm of NORTH & WATROUS, and in 1843 became the sole proprietor. Since the latter date he has had several partners, and the firm has been R. Watrous & Co., and later Watrous & Cook. In the Summer of 1862, he commenced his trade where he now is, and enjoys as a just reward for his close attention to business during twenty-four years experience here, a valuable list of friends and patrons who can always supply their wants from his store. See card, page 106.

GRIDLEY & DAVENPORT, dealers in hardware, &c., at No. 109 Water street, have been engaged in their trade here since 1842. They have a store 20 by 72; three stories and cellar, all occupied with their business, and as an instance of what attention to business combined with extensive ability and experince will accomplish, may be cited their lucrative trade and wide-spread popularity. See card, page 150.

Cook & Covell, successors to Watrous & Cook, dealers in hardware, &c., at Nos. 101 and 103 Water Street, corner Lake. Mr. E. H. Cook, the senior member of this firm, began the hardware trade in this village in 1853, as a member of the firm of R. Watrous & Co., the house having been established ten years previous to that time. In 1858, a change was made, and the firm became Watrous & Cook, and in the Summer of 1862, Mr. H. C. Covell purchased the interest of Mr. Watrous, and the present firm was formed. They occupy two stores, each 22 by 70, four stories and cellar, and the extent of their trade together with their popularity as dealers is unmistakable evidence of the fact that their patrons find their assortment complete and their prices reasonable. See card, page 60.

Few Towns in Western New York have as large a Hardware House as that of William Brown, at Nos. 14 and 16 Lake street. He commenced his present business here in 1857, as successor to H. F. Wells, and by giving his undivided attention to the interests of his trade and the wants of his patrons, has gradually increased, since his beginning, until now he occupies two stores, each 22 by 100, three stories and basement, with one of the most varied stocks of goods in his line to be found in Western New York, consisting in part of hardware, stoves, agricultural implements, tin, sheet iron and copper ware, nails, iron, cutlery, &c., &c., and his enterprise and go-ahead-a-tiveness, are rewarded by a well deserved popularity and a large trade. He is at all times prepared to supply Country Merchants at city prices. See card on outside, front cover.

In 1844 T. C. Cowen commenced trade in Elmira, and in 1858 established his auction and commission business at No. 12 Lake street, which he has conducted with marked ability and pecuniary success. In January of the present year he took as a partner, his son, Thaddeus A. Cowen, who has a good knowledge of the business, and the firm became T. C. Cowen & Son. They devote their entire attention to the purchase of good goods, at low prices and selling them proportionately low. Country Merchants and Peddlers can here find a varied assortment, from which to select. See card, page 168.

Among other branches of business conducted on a large scale in Elmira, is the grocery trade. The Wholesale House of J. H. Loring, & Co., at Nos. 166 and 168, Water street, has been doing a successful trade since its establishment in 1855, by J. H. Loring. In 1856 Mr. E. W. Hersey became a partner in the concern, and both these gentlemen have the advantage of large experience in their business, which their numerous patrons fully appreciate. Their stock is large and always well selected.

In 1856 RICHARD MORRIS commenced the grocery trade at No. 5 Lake street, and his energy and perseverance, united with his determination to please his patrons, have been well rewarded by a large and valuable trade. His store is 20 by 70, where may always be found every thing in the line of Groceries and Provisions. See card, page 108.

THOMAS BURNS has sold groceries and provisions at No. 95 Water street since the Fall of 1860, and is justly popular as a dealer. He has a store 22 by 65, at all times supplied with a complete stock of goods in his line of trade. See card, page 108.

W. J. LORMORE, grocer, at No. 25 Lake street, has conducted a successful business since his beginning in 1861. He has recently found it necessary to enlarge his store, affording him more room and better facilities for the accommodation of his constantly increasing trade, so that now he has a store 22 by 90, well stocked with groceries, provisions, wooden, willow and stone ware, &c. See card, page 64.

HARVEY SMITH, Grocer, at No. 131 Water street, opened his trade here in December, 1861, and having a thorough knowledge of his business in all its branches, has gained and well sustains a large and profitable trade. His store is 22 by 65, and his stock complete and well selected. See card, page 96.

E. WILLIAMS, Grocer &c., at No. 19 Lake street, commenced his trade here in the Spring of 1862, as a member of the firm of WILLIAMS & CARPENTER, and in January, 1863, became the sole proprietor of the business. He has a store 20 by 60, and by his attention to the wants of his patrons, fully sustains the former reputation of this justly popular establishment. He combines experience and skill with a determination to please. See card, page 76.

WILLIAM P. YATES, watchmaker and jeweler, at No. 147 Water street, commenced his trade in Elmira in 1841, and during his business experience here of more than twenty years, has gained not only a large trade by his business ability, but also, by his manner of dealing, the confidence of all his patrons. His store is 26 by 65, and his stock comprises a variety to please the most fastidious. See card, page 86.

S. AYRES, watchmaker and jeweler, and insurance agent, commenced trade here in 1844, and by managing his business with that attention to its interests, and ability, which characterize all his dealings, he has gained pecuniary success, coupled with enviable popularity as a dealer. He is the agent for Wheeler & Wilson's celebrated sewing machines, and also represents several well-known first-class fire and life insurance companies, that need no recommendation from us. See card, page 156.

At an early day in the history of this valley, about the year 1817, when Elmira was in its infancy, Mr. FRANCIS COLLINGWOOD commenced the business of watchmaker and jeweler here, which he conducted successfully during the following thirty years, and to the universal satisfaction of all his patrons. This fact may have much to do with the very flattering success which has attended his two sons, Robert and Francis, in their business here as watchmakers and jewelers, and civil engineers and surveyors, at No. 13 Lake street, which they began in 1859, as COLLINGWOOD BROTHERS, (having been engaged in the same trade during the eight years previous.) They have a store 18 by 70, and at all times keep a complete stock of goods, and their attention to business is rewarded by enviable success. They are the agents for Singer's very popular sewing machines. See card, page 116.

The house of HALL BROTHERS, booksellers, etc., at No. 128 Water street, was established in 1842, by Francis Hall, and in September 1858, passed into the hands of the present firm, who fully sustain the former enviable reputation of the house. They occupy a store 18 by 90, three stories and cellar, and reap a rich reward for their attention to business, in the way of a valuable trade. See card, page 8.

PRESWICK & DUDLEY, booksellers, etc., at No. 114 Water street. This house was established in 1845, by A. Z. Sickles, and in 1847 Mr. Preswick became his partner, and the sole proprietor in 1854. In February, 1860, Mr. Dudley became a partner of Mr. P., and the present firm was formed. They have a store 22 by 90, and by keeping up with the times in their stock, and always having a full assortment, they enjoy a liberal patronage. See card, page VI.

PERRY & SCOTT, insurance agents, at No. 103 Water street. This firm was formed in January of the present year, Mr. Perry having been a member of the firm of Lawrence & Perry, during the last two-and-a-half years, (their office having been established fifteen years,) and Mr. Scott a member of the firm of Palmer & Scott, who were the proprietors of a business established fifteen to twenty years ago. They represent fifteen first-class New York and Hartford companies, and by their prompt manner of doing business enjoy the public confidence. See card, page 154.

S. S. HUTCHINSON, manufacturer of, and dealer in boots and shoes, at No. 126 Water street, is the proprietor of a business established in

1839 by N. H. Robinson, which Mr. H. bought in February 1860, and has since that time, managed in a manner well worthy the reputation which he gained during his connection of a dozen years with the business previous to becoming the proprietor. See card, page 72.

O. B. NORTHRUP, manufacturer of, and dealer in boots and shoes, at No. 152 Water street, commenced his trade in 1859, and has met with the just reward for his prudent management and devotion to the interests of his trade. His store is 22 by 55, and his stock always composed of a complete assortment of first-class goods. To the manufacturing of work to order, he devotes much attention, using the best material and employing only the best workmen. See card, page 122.

A. L. DERBY, manufacturer of, and dealer in boots and shoes, at No. 154 Water street, commenced his present business in the spring of 1860. He has a store 22x55, and is always supplied with a good assortment of goods in his line of trade. He has, in buying eastern work, the advantage of a long personal acquaintance with the manufacturers in Massachusetts, which enables him to buy at the lowest margin of them, thereby saving a jobber's profit. See card, page 88.

The business of JOHN K. PERRY, druggist, etc., at No. 118 Water street, was established in 1835 by Tracy Beadle, and passed into the hands of the present proprietor in 1850, by whom it is conducted with success, and to the satisfaction of his patrons, he having had eighteen years experience in the drug trade. He has a store 22 by 50, and warehouse 22 by 70. Mr. P. deals largely in kerosene oils and alcohol at wholesale. See card, page 160.

JOHN D. COVELL, M. D., druggist, etc., at No. 102 Water street, commenced his trade here in the Spring of 1858, and since that time has, by uniting determination with an intimate knowledge of each department of his business, gained a good trade. He has a store 24 by 75 well arranged for the accommodation of his business. See card, page 118.

DEXTER & ELMORE, dealers in crockery, glass ware, kerosene goods, paints and oils, looking-glasses, gas-fixtures, etc., at No. 158 Water street. This house was started about the year 1850 by J. N. Elmore, and in 1858 passed into the hands of the present proprietors, who fully sustain its former well-earned reputation. They have a store 25 by 75, where may be found an almost endless variety of everything in their line of trade, and their extensive patronage is the best recommendation of the quality and prices of their goods. See card, page 84.

J. I. NICKS, tobacconist, at No. 1, Union Block, (160 Water street,) commenced his business here in 1846, and by managing it with superior ability has increased it yearly, until now his trade extends throughout Southern New York and Northern Pennsylvania, requiring him to employ twenty-five men, with as many boys and girls, in all departments, to supply his patrons. See card, page 90.

U. BARTHOLOMEW, tobacconist, at No. 9, Baldwin street, began his trade here in the Spring of 1862, and has already gained a large list of patrons by his untiring energy and perseverance in his business, in which he is much assisted by Mr. W. W. ALBRO, a gentleman of extensive experience in the business. See card, page 96.

S. B. HUBBELL, manufacturer of, and dealer in furniture, etc., and undertaker, at No. 174 Water street, has conducted a successful business in Elmira since 1841. He has a store 22 by 75 four stories high and a manufactory in the rear 18 by 28, all conveniently arranged for his business; and in its management he combines an extensive knowledge with a disposition to give his patrons the full value of their outlay. See card, page 70.

ELIASON, GREENER & Co., manufacturers of pianos, and dealers in sheet music and musical merchandise generally. Warerooms at No. 147 Water street, manufactory at No. 160 Church street. This business was begun in 1854 by the present proprietors, Mr. Eliason the senior member of the firm having been in the music trade here during the four years previous. Their manufactory is complete in all its fixtures, and these gentlemen have an intimate knowledge of their business. That they make superior instruments is attested by numerous letters from eminent artists, among whom are M. Gottschalk, M. Strakosch, S. B. Mills, Edward Hoffman, Madame Anna Bishop, and many others. See card, page 86.

ELMIRA MILLS, SAMUEL HOTCHKIN proprietor, on Water street, near College avenue, were built in 1828, 40 front by 60 feet deep. In 1860 two additions were made, one on the eastern side 60 feet front by 30 deep, and one on the western side, 20 feet front by 40 deep, making the whole building now 120 feet front and three stories high. They have four runs of stone and are capable of manufacturing 300 barrels of flour per day, of a superior quality. In May, 1861, the present proprietor, Mr. Hotchkin leased these Mills, and the ability and energy which he displays in the conducting of his business has gained for him the well merited confidence of the entire community. See card, page 158

ELMIRA.

ARNOT MILLS, located at the east end of Water street, C. F. West proprietor, were erected in 1836, by Stephen Tuttle, and in 1850 or thereabouts, became the property of Mrs. John Arnot. They were leased by Mr. West in the Fall of 1857. They are 40 by 60, three stories high and have four runs of stone, capable of manufacturing 120 barrels of Flour per day, besides a large quantity of Corn Meal, Feed, &c. The manner in which Mr. West manages all his transactions, and the quality of his work has gained for him a large patronage which he well sustains. See card, page 167.

ELMIRA STEAM MILLS, W. HALLIDAY & Co., proprietors. These mills were erected in 1850 by A. C. Ely, on the corner of Baldwin and Carroll streets, removed to their present location on Basin street in 1857, and purchased by the present proprietors in the Summer of 1861. They have four runs of stone and can manufacture fifty barrels of flour per day, besides other grains. The ready sale which the flour from these mills meets with in the market is its best recommendation. See card, page 62.

S. R. VAN CAMPEN, banker and exchange broker, on the corner of Water and Baldwin streets, (Brainard Block,) commenced his business here in 1859, and by the manner in which he conducts it and the ability which he displays in all his dealings has gained the confidence of the entire business community. His Banking House is the depository for the United States Internal Revenue Stamps.

RATHBUN'S BRAINARD HOUSE, C. SLATER, proprietor, situated on the corner of Water and Baldwin streets. This house was erected in 1850, is 100 feet on Water and 200 feet on Baldwin, six stories high including the basement, has eighty rooms, besides commodious office, reading-room, parlors, &c., and a model dining hall, capable of seating 300 persons. The present proprietor, Mr. Slater, who has done the catering for this popular house during the last three years, leased it in May, 1862, and became "Mine Host," and with his well deserved and widely known reputation, his name gave "The Brainard" additional popularity, which is well sustained and daily increasing. See card on outside of back cover.

E. B. SMITH, baker and confectioner and dealer in variety goods, at No. 1, Brainard Block, commenced his trade here in 1858, since which time he has gained a wide spread popularity. His store is 20 by 50, and he has a manufactory on Basin street 36 by 45, and the enviable reputation which he enjoys as a dealer taxes his facilities to their utmost capacity for the supplying of his trade. See card, page 118.

LEVI COKE, baker and confectioner, No. 31 Lake street, commenced his business in 1858. He has a store 25 by 80 and has a very extensive experience in his business which enables him to please all his patrons. See card, page 166.

W. MERWIN, manufacturer of and dealer in harness, saddles, trunks, &c., at No. 141, Water street, has been engaged in his business here during the last twenty-five years, and by employing in his manufacturing only the most competent workmen and using first class stock, he has gained a reputation which gives him a valuable list of customers. See card, page 88.

J. M. TILLMAN, harness maker, &c., at No. 41 Lake street, commenced his trade here in 1859. He has a store 25 by 100, and his long experience in the business gives him a large share of the public patronage. See card, page 110.

H. W. MCINTIRE, manufacturer of Johnson's Patent Shingle Machine, at No. 12 Wisner street. This machine was first introduced to public notice in 1850, since which time over one thousand have been sold in the United States and Canadas. Mr. M. is a practical machinist and superintends the construction of each machine. See card, page 110.

THE UNION COFFEE MILLS, G. H. POST, proprietor, were established in 1859 by Fielding & Ferguson, and in January, 1862, Mr. Post became a partner of Mr. Fielding, and in January, 1863, the sole proprietor. He has two stores, each 22 by 80, three stories and cellar, except one office on the second floor, all occupied with his business. He deals extensively at wholesale and retail in coffees, teas and spices of all kinds, and the extent of his trade well attests that he fully sustains the former enviable reputation of this house. See card, page 82.

G. W. WATERS, portrait and landscape painter, at No. 135 Water street, commenced his profession in Elmira in the Spring of 1861, since which time he has given much evidence of his skill as an artist. An examination of the pictures in his studio, works of his own, will convince that his taste in design, and skill in execution, cannot be surpassed in the Empire State, and the publisher with pleasure refers to his card on page 142.

A. P. HART, photographer, at No. 22 Lake street, commenced the picture business in Elmira in 1837, conducted it successfully until 1840, when he removed from the village. In 1842 he again opened rooms here, which he operated until 1855, when he sold them, and in 1861 again established himself at his present location, where with his former reputation he at once commanded a large patronage which is well deserved. See card, outside front cover.

W. J. MOULTON, photographer and stock dealer, at Nos. 116 and 118 Water street, established his present business here in 1855, and has pleased his patrons so well by his success in making good pictures, a result of the employment of an intimate knowledge of the business, united with a determination to succeed, that he now has an extensive and profitable business and a justly deserved reputation for excelling in his line. In his room he has numerous portraits of distinguished persons, from all parts of the world, and an examination of these well repays the visitor.

G. W. SCARDEFIELD & Co., gilders, and manufacturers of looking-glass and picture frames, at No. 11 Baldwin street. This concern was established about five years ago by Mr. Scardefield, and in the Fall of 1861 Mr. A. P. ROOSA became connected with the business. They manufacture all kinds of looking-glass and picture frames of a superior style of workmanship, and at prices to please their patrons. See card, page 74.

T. S. PATTINSON, butcher, and oyster dealer, at No. 123 Water street, has been in business in Elmira during the last twenty-five years, and now enjoys, as a result of his many years of application to business, coupled with liberality and fair dealing, a large patronage, and has the satisfaction of knowing that he is a popular dealer. See card, page 64.

A reliable painter, and one who attends to his business and pleases his patrons, is the well-known WASH. MARSH, at Nos. 5 and 6, Union Block. Mr. Marsh commenced his business here seven years ago, and long since gained a reputation that needs no recommendation from us. His knowledge of his business is thorough and complete, in all its branches, and he adds good execution to tasty designing. See card, page 98.

Dr. T. S. UP DE GRAFF, oculist and aurist, at No. 151 Water street, located himself here for the practice of his profession, in the Fall of 1862, and his success, together with the constant increase of his practice, sufficiently evidences his superior skill. All persons afflicted with any disease of the eye or ear, cannot do better than to call at Dr. U's office. See card, page 102.

ARBOUR HOTEL, saloon, restaurant, and billiard-rooms, at Nos. 7, 9, and 11 Lake street, Joshua Jones, proprietor. This popular establishment was opened in 1849 by G. M. & H. B. Jones, in a wooden building occupying the site of their present location. In 1852, the building which it now occupies was erected, and a portion of it fitted up under their supervision, expressly for their trade. In 1858 the present proprietor purchased the business of the Arbour, and by his attention to his patrons, has become exceedingly popular. See card, page 74.

OWEN MCGREEVY's livery, corner of Lake and Cross streets, has become one of the popular institutions of Elmira, since its establishment in 1849. Mr. McGreevy keeps from 20 to 30 horses, with a full assortment of carriages, and careful-drivers; and the facilities of this first-class establishment are taxed to the utmost. See card, page 124.

CRANS. T. POTTER, livery-man, on Carroll street, between Baldwin and Lake, commenced his business in Elmira in 1858, and during his five years experience here, has gained many friends among those who are fond of driving good horses. He keeps from 12 to 15 horses, with a full complement of carriages, and all the appurtenances of a first-class establishment. See card, page 4.

CRANS. T. POTTER,

LIVERY,

CARROLL ST.,

Between Baldwin and Lake, Elmira, N. Y.

THE BEST OF HORSES, WITH FIRST CLASS CARRIAGES, TO

LET ON REASONABLE TERMS

THE ELMIRA ADVERTISER,

ELMIRA, N. Y.

S. B. FAIRMAN, - - - PROPRIETOR.

S. B. FAIRMAN & C. G. FAIRMAN, Editors.

Published Daily & Weekly at Nos. 8 & 10 Lake Street,

TERMS.---DAILY, 10 Cents a Week or $5,00 a Year.
" WEEKLY, $1.50 a Year in advance, or $2.00 a Year for arrears.

The ADVERTISER sustains cordially the Administration of President Lincoln, in all its measures for the suppression of the slaveholders' rebellion and the preservation of the Union. It holds that armed rebellion against the Government must be put down by the strong hand of power, and that the Administration has a right to use, for this purpose, every recognized weapon of warfare ; to command the zealous support of all loyal citizens and to summarily suppress all disloyal manifestations. It holds, also, that Justice is Policy, and the progress of humanity the legitimate object of philanthropic effort, and therefore claims the right to rejoice if the wicked attempt to destroy the Union in behalf of Slavery shall result in the destruction of that Barbarism itself, and the more permanent and universal guaranty of the right of all to life, liberty and the pursuit of happines.

The ADVERTISER is now in its tenth year, and has an establised circulation superior to that of any other paper in Chemung County, which renders it one of the best mediums for Advertising in the "Southern Tier."

ELMIRA
DAILY PRESS.

MORNING PAPER.

THE LARGEST CIRCULATION OF ANY PAPER IN THE "SOUTHERN TIER."

PRINTING OF EVERY DESCRIPTION

Executed with Neatness and Dispatch at the

Elmira Daily Press

Book & Job Printing Establishment,

Corner Lake and Water-Sts, at the shortest Notice, and at the lowest CASH prices.

WE possess unequaled facilities for the prompt execution of LAW CASES and POINTS, as well as LAW BLANKS of all descriptions; Summonses, Complaints, Notices of Object of Action, Demurrers, Opinions, Decrees, Injunctions, &c., &c. &c. Also, Books and Pamphlets, Abstracts of Title, Policies of Insurance, Cards, Circulars, Notes, Bill Heads, Catalogues, Bank Checks, Receipts, Show Cards, Posters, Programmes, Tickets, Hotel Registers, &c., &c.

THAYER & WHITLEY, Propr's.

THE DAILY PRESS
BOOK BINDERY

Has facilities for executing all orders that can be brought for work in that line. MAGAZINES, PERIODICALS, MUSIC, &c., bound in the highest style of art, as also every kind and style of Binding which may be wanted, in the latest and most approved styles, and on reasonable terms. All work warranted. All kinds of GILT WORK will be executed in the best manner. OLD BOOKS re-bound and made as good as new.

CITY BOOKSTORE,

No. 114 Water St., Elmira, N. Y.

PRESWICK & DUDLEY

Offer unusual inducements to the purchasers of

Books, Stationery, Wall-Paper,

and all other goods within the range of the Bookseller's trade. Their Stock includes full supplies of

School, Miscellaneous, Law and Medical Books;

Publications of the Sunday School Union, American Tract Society, Bible Society, and all other leading Religious Book Concerns.

ENGLISH, FRENCH AND AMERICAN

STATIONERY,

Writing, Printing & Wrapping Papers

OF ALL SIZES AND QUALITIES.

BLANK BOOKS OF EVERY DESCRIPTION,

Including those used by Banking and Mercantile Houses, Circuit and County Courts, Railroad Offices, &c.

LAW BLANKS, for use in Supreme, County and Justices Courts.

PAPER HANGINGS & BORDERS, FIRE-BOARD VIEWS, WINDOW PAPERS, GOLD, METAL, PLAIN AND OIL SHADES, in wonderful variety. Their stock of these goods is as large, well chosen and CHEAP as any in Southern New York.

PRINTERS' CARDS AND CARD BOARD-----WHITE, COLORED, ENAMELED AND IVORY.

Sheet Music, Violin & Guitar Strings.

PHOTOGRAPH ALBUMS.

Cartes-de-Visite of distinguished personages; Steel Engravings, Colored Prints, Gilt Frames, Willow Baskets, Traveling Bags, Portfolios, Porte-Monnaies, Gold Pens, Writing Desks, &c., &c., &c.

Orders for Foreign or American Publications attended to with promptness. The highest price, in Cash or Trade, paid for Rags.

C. PRESWICK.   JAMES T. DUDLEY.

ESTABLISHED 1842.

The Cheap Cash Bookstore,

—OF—

HALL BROTHERS,

Where can always be found a well selected Stock of

Miscellaneous & Standard Books,

INCLUDING ALL THE

LATEST PUBLICATIONS OF THE DAY.

ANY FOREIGN OR AMERICAN BOOK PROCURED TO ORDER.

SCHOOL BOOKS

of every variety used in this section.

BLANK BOOKS of superior quality constantly in stock or made to suit, of any size, shape or style of ruling.

CAP, LETTER AND NOTE PAPERS, WITH ENVELOPES AND STATIONERY in all its branches.

Wrapping Papers, Wall Papers, Decorations, Borders, Fire Board Views, and Curtain Papers,

GILT & PLAIN WINDOW SHADES.

Buff-Holland, Picture Tassels and Cords,

The largest Assortment in Southern New York.

A Select Assortment of Fancy Articles.

Sole Depository of the American Bible Society for Chemung County. Agency of the American Tract Societies and American S. S. Union.

It is the aim of the subscribers to offer none but good articles, and those at a moderate price. Our motto is

"NEVER UNDER SOLD."

FREDERIC HALL.   CHARLES C. HALL.   ROBERT A. HALL.

HISTORY OF ELMIRA

BY

HON. THOMAS MAXWELL.

The Village of Elmira, (by its original name of Newtown or Newtown Point,) was first laid out on a lot of land granted to Jeffrey Wisner, on Newtown Creek, where the first buildings were erected about the year 1790, on what is now known as Sullivan Street. The residence of Doctor Hinchman, Doctor Scott, Vincent Mathews, Peter Loop, and Christian Loop, were built on Sullivan Street. Shortly afterwards the Old Court House was built. It was a two story building of hewn logs, well clapboarded—the lower part used as a jail and as a dwelling for the Jailer—the second floor as a Court Room and a place of public worship, and the Attic as a Masonic Lodge. Before the erection of the Old Court House, a Court of Oyer and Terminer was held at the Public House of Dunn & Hornell, on Sullivan Street, (called the Stoner House, near Newtown Creek, and now torn down) in July 1794, by Judge Benson, of the Supreme Court, assisted by Justices Mersereau, Abraham Miller and John Miller. The precise time of the occupation of the Sullivan Street Court House does not appear, as the records of the Courts are not to be found, but it is supposed to have been in 1796. Within its unassuming walls have sat those judicial luminaries of the State, Benson, Hobart, Livingston, Spencer, Kent, Van Ness, Platt, Thompson, Yates, Woodworth, Tompkins, and others, of that splendid corps of Jurists, who have placed New York so high on the roll of judicial excellence, and whose decisions have attained universal credence on the American continent. The writer has a vivid recollection of the ceremonies of escorting a "Supreme Judge," from Dunn's Tavern, (on the corner of Lake and Water Streets,) to the Old Court House. The Sheriff, wearing a cocked hat, of the old Continental stamp, a drawn sword in his hand, his corps of Constables, with long staves, preceded by martial music; the judges arm in arm, followed by the bar, carrying their green bags, for briefs and papers, witnesses, jurors and parties closing the procession, made a most imposing appearance. The veneration with which these judicial lights were looked upon by the people, and the implicit faith, which held their decisions to be the end of the law, is also well remembered.

Not a vestige of the old Court House, which stood on the Corner of Church and Sullivan Streets, as now arranged, remains; but its walls have reverberated with the eloquent appeals and sound legal lore of Mathews, Howell, Haight, Wisner, Dana, Johnson, Woodcock, Strong, Sedgwick, Avery, Sherwood, Spencer, Collier, Konkle, and many others, of the legal fraternity who attended our Courts. There are those among us who remember the old building and the many purposes to which it was devoted, who can recall many interesting incidents which occurred within its humble walls, which will remain among their cherished memories while they linger upon earth. Since the organization of Chemung the Courts have been held in the building which stood on the site of the present splendid structure, and which has been removed and fitted up as a Town Hall, by the Village Trustees, and which reflects so much credit upon their public spirit. The first judges who have presided in the County Courts, since the organization of Chemung, are Joseph L. Darling, James Dunn, John W. Wisner, A. S. Thurston, Theodore North, Aaron Konkle, H. Boardman Smith, and the present incumbent, Hon. E. P. Brooks. Grant B. Baldwin, a member of the bar and resident of Elmira, was the first Judge of Tioga. Among the District Attorneys of the County were, A. Konkle, Wm. Maxwell, A. K. Gregg, E. Quin, A. Robertson, H. Gray, D. C. Woodcock, Wm. North, E. P. Hart, E. P. Brooks, S. B. Tomlinson, and John Murdoch, Esquires.

In Dec. 1794, Guy Maxwell, then of Tioga Point, and Samuel Hepburn, of Milton, Pa., purchased of Thomas White, Lot. No. 1 of Great Lot No. 195, containing 100 acres, for the sum of five hundred pounds. or $12.50 per acre; and laid out a Town Plot on the river bank, the site of the present village. The plot was called DeWittsburgh on the map and in the conveyances. At the same time Henry Wisner, Esq., of Warwick, Orange Co., who owned lot No. 196, west of DeWitt's patent, laid out his town plot which was called Wisnerburgh. The dividing line between their patents was a little west of the street now called Baldwin street. These names, however, were not generally adopted, but the village continued to be called Newtown until the name of the town was changed by the Legislature to Elmira, in 1811.

The village had been incorporated by the name of Newtown, in March 1815, and a subsequent act, April 21, 1828, changed it to Elmira.

The town of Newtown was erected April 10, 1792, it having previously been within the limits of the Town of Chemung. Catharine was taken from Elmira in 1798; Big Flatts and Southport in 1822, and Horseheads in 1854. The village is handsomely situated on the north bank of the Chemung, now divided into the First and Second Wards; and recently a Third Ward on the South side of the river, in the town of Southport, has been included within its corporate bounds. Upon a high hill west of the village, called Fort Hill, is the remains of an ancient fortification, protected on the northerly side by the river at the base of the hill, and on the southerly side by a deep ravine, through which passes a stream falling into the river. An embankment two hundred feet long and fourteen feet wide and three and a half feet high still extends along the rear of the fortification on the west, and upon it grew large trees when the whites first occupied the country. Col. Hendy, one of the earliest settlers, frequently stated that he had enquired of the older Indians, then in the neighborhood, as to the object of this embankment, and by whom erected; but they could give no information on the subject nor did they have any tradition in reference to it.

The earliest merchant who had a trading establishment here was Col. Matthias Hollenback, of Wilkesbarre, whose establishment was first located at the junction of the creek with the river, and was under the charge of Capt. Daniel McDowell, who was succeeded by John Morris. Afterwards Col. Hollenback removed his establishment farther up the river, where for many years it was under charge of Archibald Campbell, George Denison, John Cherry and Matthew McReynolds and Bela B. Hyde. Mr. Hollenback had a trading establishment at Tioga Point, (now Athens, Pa.,) which was in charge of Guy Maxwell from 1788 to 1796, when he removed to Elmira, and was succeeded by John Alexander, who about the year 1800, was succeeded by the late Stephen Tuttle, who in connection with Mr. Robert Covell, commenced busidess in Elmira in 1807, and for many years carried on a profitable business, having the entire confidence and respect of their customers. Mr. Tuttle came to Elmira in 1818. Howes Goldsborough was among the old merchants; Guy Maxwell, Thomas M. Perry, James Irwin, Michael Pfautz, Ephraim Heller, Lyman Covell, Miles Covell, Isaac Baldwin, John Cherry, John Hollenback, Thomas Maxwell, Samuel H. Maxwell, Isaac Reynolds and others. John Arnot, now Prest. of the Chemung Canal Bank, commenced business here as a merchant in the Winter or Spring of 1819. He has amassed a princely fortune by strict attention to business and careful and prudent management. His reputation as a correct business man and accommodating merchant is not surpassed by any of the old merchants. Maj. Horatio Ross kept a mercantile establishment for a number of years, and was universally appreciated as a man of probity and honor, and no place in the Southern Tier can boast of more honest, upright merchants than Elmira. [The more recent mercantile establishments will be noticed hereafter.]

Among the old Lawyers who have resided in Elmira, not already mentioned, were Peter Loop, David Jones, Samuel S. Haight, Wm. Lowe, George C. Edwards, Peter Masterton, William Wisner, James Robinson, Aaron Konkle, Theodore and Wm. North, Theodore North, Jr. Hiram Gray, Andrew K. Gregg, James Dunn, Grant B. Baldwin, William Maxwell, Wm. P. Konkle, E. P. Brooks, S. G. Hathaway, Jr., A. S. Diven, John W. Wisner, A. S. Thurston, Thos. Maxwell, and among those more recent and yet in practice, Archibald Robertson, N. P. Fassett, E. P. Hart, Edw'd Quinn, John Murdoch, E. H. Benn, Simeon Rood, G. M. Diven, S. B. Tomlinson, R. H. Ransom, D. B. Smith, S. C. Reynolds, U. S. Lowe, D. W. Gillet, Rufus King, G. L. Davis, G. A. Brush, J. R. Ward, James DeWitt, J. H. Hardy.

Among the Physicians who were among the most prominent in the village, were Joseph Hinchman, Amos Park, Christian Schott, J. Chamberlain, John Ross, James Ross, A. G. White, Dr. Aspinwall, R. Bancroft, J. Purdy, Theseus Brooks, and those of more recent date will be found elsewhere.

As the first settlers were very many of them in Sullivan's Expedition against the Six Nations of Indians in 1779, and hence became acquainted with the rich vallies of Chemung and Susquehanna, some notice of his expedition would seem to be necessary.

The terrible Indian massacre at Wyoming, in 1778, (July 3d,) and other offences committed against the defenceless inhabitants of the various frontiers, seemed to demand this terrible retribution—as terrible it was. Many philanthropists have considered this punishment as too great for ignorant savages; but the affair was planned and approved by Wasnington himself. No border settler whose relatives had been victims to the terrible scalping-knife felt any compunction in reference to the destruction of the crops and fruit-trees, in this expedition of Sullivan's, and few of their descendants at this day can be found to call the punishment of the Indians cruel and vindictive. Nor do any of the Indians of the present age, nor did those of the past, permit this expedition to lessen in any degree their veneration for Washington. Indeed, the new system of religion adopted among the Seneca's has a most beautiful exemplification of their veneration for the father of his country, whose cognomen after 1779 was universal among the various tribes, to-wit; Hanodagarears, or Town-destroyer. One of the tenets engrafted upon the ancient Indian faith relates to Washington—according to their belief no white man ever reached the Indian Heaven except Washington—whose justice and benevolence stands pre-eminent among them. It represents him as located at the entrance of the happy hunting grounds, within a spacious building constructed like a fort, surrounded by every object which could gratify a cultivated taste. The faithful Indian who enters Heavan passes this enclosure. He sees and recognizes the illustrious inmate, who is walking in quiet meditation in the shady groves, in full uniform. No one ever speaks to him, but all pass in respectful silence.

Such is the monument which Indian gratitude has erected to Washington, who came to their aid when, by the treaty of peace with England, in 1783, no provision was made by the British for their Indian allies, but left them to the mercy of the American Government. Washington was their fast friend during his presidency, and the Indians appreciate his kindly efforts in their behalf, and have thus shown their veneration for his memory.

On the first of May 1779, the Second and Fourth New-York Regiments left their camp near the Hudson and passing through Warwarsing arrived upon the Delaware on the ninth. They crossed the Delaware and passed down the west side to Easton, at which place their stores were collected. From thence they marched toward Wyoming, where they arrived on the 17th June. The delay was occasioned by the great labor required to open a road through woods and over an almost impassable swamp extending many miles. General Sullivan arrived with the main army on the 24th. On the 31st July, the army left Wyoming for the Indian settlements. The stores and artillery were conveyed up the Susquehanna in 150 boats. " The boats formed a beautiful appearance as they moved in order from their moorings, and as they passed the fort received a grand salute, which was returned by the loud cheers of the boatmen. The whole scene formed a military display surpassing any which had ever been exhibited at Wyoming ; and was well calculated to form a powerful impression upon the minds of those lurking parties of savages which still continued to roam upon the mountains, from which all their movements were visible for many miles."

On the 11th of August they arrived at Tioga, now Athens, and encamped on the forks of the river. On the 12th a detachment was sent forward to Chemung, twelve miles distant, where they were attacked by a body of Indians, and lost seven men kiled and wounded. The next day, having burned the town, (this was on McDowell's flats,) they returned to Tioga.

About a mile and a quarter above the junction of the Tioga (or Chemung) and Susquehanna, these rivers approach within a stone's throw. Here a fort was built called Fort Sullivan, while the army lay on what might almost be called an island below.

In this situation Gen. Sullivan awaited the arrival of Gen. Clinton. This officer, with the 1st and 3d New York Regiments, passed up the Mohawk to Canajoharie, where he arrived early in the Spring. An expedition was sent from here by Gen. Clinton against the Onondaga Indians. General Clinton commenced opening a road from Canajoharie to the head of Otsego lake, distant about twenty miles, and one of the principal sources of the eastern branch of the Susquehanna. This was effected with great labor. His boats were carried across in wagons. It was mid-Summer before General Clinton found himself with his army and baggage at the head of the lake, upon which he launched his boats.

This is a beautiful lake about nine miles long, and varies in width from one to three miles. Its elevation is 1193 feet, and it is almost surrounded by high land. The water is *deep and clear*, which is said to be the meaning of its Indian name, *Otsego*. Its outlet is narrow.

Gen. Clinton having passed his boats through, caused a dam to be thrown across the outlet. The lake was raised several feet. A party was sent forward to clear the river of drift-wood. When ready to move, the dam was broken up and the boats glided swiftly down the current. The few scattered inhabitants along the river below fled in dismay, being unable to account for the sudden rise of the river when no rains had fallen. At Tioga, the water flowed back up the western branch.

On the 22d of August, this division arrived at Tioga and joined the main army. The whole force now under Gen. Sullivan consisted of the brigades of Generals Hand, Maxwell, Clinton and Poor, Proctor's Artillery and a corps of Riflemen, in all between four and five thousand men. On the 26th, this army, formidable indeed, if the numbers of the enemy be considered, moved from Tioga, up the river of that name, (now called Chemung) in excellent order. Their progress was necessarily slow, and every precaution was taken to guard against surprise. Large flanking parties were kept out on each side, and a corps of light troops was thrown forward. On the 28th they destroyed the settlements and grain at Chemung, and on the morning of the 29th August, about ten o'clock fell in with the enemy near Newtown, and a short distance from the mouth of Butler's creek, (now called Baldwin's creek.) They were under the Butlers and Brant, and were in number about 600 Indians and 200 Tories. After some reconnoitering and skirmishing, the enemy retreated behind their breastwork and made a spirited resistance. They were soon driven from their position by the artillery. In the meantime the brigades of Clinton and Poor filed off to the right, and Gen. Hand's light troops to the left, to gain the rear of the enemy where the land was high. Had this been effected the enemy could not have escaped; but the movement is said to have been discovered by Brant, who ordered an immediate retreat. Nine Indians were left dead on the field; their wounded and many of their dead were carried off. The Americans lost in killed, three; thirty-four were wounded, among whom were Maj. Titcomb, Capt. Clayes, Lieut. McCally (who died of his wounds,) and Ensign Thomas Baldwin. Two prisoners were taken who gave information of the force of the enemy. This was the only stand made by the Indians. When it was first announced that an army was marching into their country, the Indians laughed at at their supposed folly, believing it impossible for a regular army to traverse the wilderness such a distance, and to drive them from their fastnesses. The manuscript journal of Col. Gansevoort, of Clinton's brigade, has the following remarks:

"1779, August 29.—This night encamped on the field of battle. 30th—Remained on the ground; large detachments sent off this morning to destroy the corn, beans, &c., about this place, which was not half done. This evening sent off our wounded, heavy artillery and wagons down the river to Tioga; these boats brought forward such stores as could not be loaded on pack-horses. This day put on half allowance.

31st Aug., decamped at 8 o'clock—marched over mountainous ground until we arrived at the forks of Newtown,—(this was where the Newtown Creek, as now called, falls into the river below Elmira Village,) there entered on a low bottom; crossed the Kayuga branch (now Newtown Creek,) and encamped on a pine plain,—much good land about Newtown. Here we left the Tioga branch to our left.

Sept. 1st, decamped early in the morning; marched about three miles and entered a swamp eight or nine miles across,—roads very bad and no pasture here. The army made a forced march and arrived that night at dark in Catharine's Town."

The journal continues to detail the daily events of the expedition until it arrives at Genessee River, near Rochester; from whence, after destroying the corn, &c., on the Genesee Flats, they returned toward the Tioga or Chemung River. These details are omitted, though highly interesting. The journal continues—

" Sept. 24, passed the swamp (Catharine Swamp) so much dreaded from its badness, without any difficulty, and arrived at the forks of Newtown, where Capt. Reid with a detachment of two hundred men had thrown up a breast work to guard some stores and cattle brought forward from Tioga for the army in case of necessity. Saluted by thirteen rounds of cannon from the breastwork on our arrival, which number we returned from our artillery.

25th Sept. This morning the small arms of the whole army were discharged. At 5 o'clock they were drawn up in one line, with a field-piece on the right of each brigade to a fire *feu de joie*. 1st, thirteen rounds of cannon. 2d, a running fire of musketry from right to left, which was repeated twice. Five oxen were killed on this joyous occasion—one delivered to each brigade, and one to the artillery and staff. This was done in consequence of the Declaration of War by Spain against Great Britain, the news of which reached the army here.

They remained here waiting the return of the detachments which had been sent to destroy the villages, grain and fruit trees on either side of the Cayuga Lake, and to destroy the crops on the river about Elmira and Big Flats.

The army finally decamped from Newtown Point on the 28th of September and arrived at Fort Sullivan on the 30th. On the 3d of October the fort was demolished, and the army returned by way of Wyoming and Easton, where it arrived on the 13th.

The whole distance from Easton to the Genesee Castle by the route of the army was 280 miles. The loss of men in this expedition was inconsiderable, considering the fatigue and exposure, not more than forty in the whole were killed or died from sickness. The breast work thrown up by Captain Reid referred to, was along the bank of the Newtown Creek, as far up as where the highway now crosses the bridge below Sullivan Mills, then running westwardly on the South side of the road some sixty or eighty rods thence to the river, and down the river to the mouth of the creek, enclosing an area of three or four acres, and enclosed all around by palisades. Traces of the embankment from the river northwardly to the highway are yet visible.

The name of the river is given in the journal of Col. Ganesvoort as the Tioga. It has since been called the Chemung—and it is said it was so called from a large horn having been found in the river near Bydelman's, by the Indians—Chemung meaning great horn. The Muncies and Delawares called it Conongue, which in their language means horn in the water. A similar horn was found in the water at the lower end of the Upper Narrows, by some of the early settlers. Captain Daniel McDowell, a former resident of Chemung was captured at Shawanee on the 12th of September, 1782, by the Indians, and carried to Niagara, and thence to Quebec. While a captive among the Indians he saw (it is believed at Quebec,) the identical horn which gave the name of Chemung to the river theretofore called Tioga. He stated to the writer in his life time that it was a counterpart of the one found at the Upper Narrows, about the year 1791. Captain McDowell had seen both, and was well calculated to give an opinion in the matter. The river is still called Tioga above its junction with the Cohocton, at Painted Post, and to its head, in the neighborhood of Blossburgh, Pennsylvania.

The portions of the Iroquois tribes, who occupied the country between the Chemung River and the Seneca Lake, were at the period of Sullivan's expedition in 1779, principally Seneca's, Cayuga's and Tuscarora's. After the battle of Newtown, Aug. 1779, they seem to have made very little resistance to the army of Sullivan. The Indian King Canadesaga, who is said to have been a Seneca, was killed at that battle. It is said he was the husband of the celebrated Catharine Montour.

When the country was first settled, between 1787 and 1790, there were many families of Indians between the river and the lake, which was common hunting ground, free to all the tribes of the Six Nations. There were then in Elmira, three villages of Indian cabins—one between Main street and the Baptist Church of thirty or forty cabins; another on the flats near the Creek, now owned by Mrs. Arnot, called Kan-a-we-o-la; and the third on the east side of the Creek below the Water Cure. These families left the country about 1802, when the small pox made fearful ravages among them, and the survivors fled further west. Some of their descendants are still found near Batavia. They produced many distinguished men, some of whom were well known to the early settlers—none more distinguished than Sa-go-ye-wa-tha, the celebrated Red Jacket. He exhibited great powers of oratory at the treaty held with the tribes by Colonel Pickering, at Newtown Point, in 1791.

The object of the Government was to induce them to become agriculturalists, (a favorite project of Gen. Washington,) and on that occasion very liberal offers were made to them by Pickering. Red

Jacket who had always opposed every attempt to civilize or Christianize them, exhibited on this occasion his greatest powers of mind, in opposition to the propositions of the Government. This effort was represented by Jasper Parrish, who attended the treaty as an interpreter, to have been the greatest he ever heard from the eloquent chief—and the result was that the proposals were rejected by all but Cornplanter's tribe.

To one, who saw much of him in his later years, when he was evidently on the wane, and the "fire-water"—the bane of all the tribes—had left its traces, visibly, upon his mind and person, he stated in 1828, that when a child, he accompanied his relatives to a great Council of the Tribes, held on the Shenandoah, in Virginia, near Harper's Ferry. That the various nations were represented by their most able men, but that the greatest among them all was Logan, a Cayugan, who had left his residence on the banks of the Cayuga, for Shamokin, on the Susquehanna. His father, Shikellimo, was held in high estimation by the Pennsylvania authorities, and was much esteemed by James Logan the Secretary of State, for whom the chief was named. Red Jacket remarked that he was so highly delighted with the eloquence of Logan, that he resolved to devote himself to public speaking, and to follow Logan as his model. He stated that after his return to the banks of the Crooked Lake, —the residence of his parents—he frequently incurred the reproofs of his mother for his long-continued absences from her cabin, without any ostensible cause; and when hard pressed for an answer, would reply that he had been "playing Logan." He said that he was in the habit of repairing to the woods, or where he could find a waterfall, where he exercised his voice amid the roaring waters, to acquire the necessary command and tone to address large assemblies, and that through life he had endeavored to acquire the manner and style of Logan.

One of his favorite resorts for this purpose, was at the head of the magnificent water-fall at Havana, (as it was, before a portion of its waters were diverted for practical purposes.) The name of the stream was She-qua-gah, or as he interpreted it, "the place of the roaring waters." The water-fall seems to have been his peculiar inspiration. When called upon by Captain Eastman for his portrait to adorn the pages of Schoolcraft's great work on Indian History, recently published by the Government, he declined, unless it were taken at Niagara with the Falls in the back-ground. He is represented in the picture as seated upon a rock, on the American side, in full costume, with his war-pipe in his hand and his face to the setting sun, while on his right, the "tumbling waters are rushing over the precipice at his feet." In early life, the beautiful She-qua-gah, and in his mature years, the mighty Ne-au-ga-rah, (his own pronunciation of the word,) were his favorite haunts. What better surroundings need be required to draw forth the mighty spirit of eloquence which characterized the man? Thus, unconsciously, was this celebrated forest orator an imitator of the eloquent Greek, who tuned his voice on the sea-beach, while he caught his inspiration from the altar of Nature.— From this revelation of the eloquent Chief, it is evident that his power of swaying the multitude, was acquired by long and laborious preparation in the depths of the forest. How near he approached Logan, (his celebrated model,) in attitude, gesture and intonation, cannot now be told, as no one now lives who has heard them both. That he was a profound though unlettered student of oratory, is abundantly testified by those who heard him in his palmiest days.

Of the "Speech of Logan," which has given him a world-wide reputation, and is familiar to every school-boy in the land, Mr. Jefferson says "I may challenge the whole Orations of Demosthenes and Cicero and of any more eminent orator, if Europe has furnished more eminent, to produce a single passage superior to the speech of Logan." The citizens of Auburn have, much to their credit, erected a monument to his memory on Fort Allegan, near their city, which bears this expression from his celebrated speech:—"Who is there to mourn for Logan? Not one!"

In Harpers' N. Y. & Erie Rail Road Guide, a great many very singular mistakes occur. He states that Elmira was settled in 1788 by Capt. JOHN HENDY. Col. HENDY settled three miles above the village about that period. He says that Col. Hendy *anglicised* the Indian name to *Newton*. This is another error—Col. H. never gave the name to the place. It was called *Newtown Point*, in the first settlement of the country. There were two Indian towns destroyed by Sullivan— one on the Chemung Flatts, near Buckville, which was called Old Chemung or *Old Town*, and the other on the Baldwin & Lowman Flatts, near the line between the towns of Chemung and Elmira, which was called New Chemung or *Newtown*; and when Elmira began to be settled it was called Newtown Point, though five miles above the spot where the Indian village stood. From the neighborhood of this Indian village, Sullivan's engagement with the Indians was called the battle of Newtown. The battle ground is a little north of Baldwin's Creek, where the road passes, near Baldwin's Mills, and was on land formerly owned by Col. Isaac Baldwin, and on a part of the farm now owned by Jesse Carpenter. The writer passed over the battle ground many years ago, when all the localities were pointed out by Col. Thomas Baldwin and Major Waterman Baldwin, both of whom were in the battle; the former was wounded. Col. Stone seems to have fallen into the same error. Soon after the publication of his Life of Brant, his attention was called to the error, and the writer proposed visiting the battle ground in company with him. He appointed the anniversary of the battle as the day of the visit, August 29th. He came as far as the head of Seneca Lake, where, being suddenly taken ill, he wrote to his correspondent postponing the visit to the same day in the next year, but he died at Saratoga the following summer, and he never visited the battle ground. Two persons were ready to meet him who were in the battle—John Fitz Simmons and Daniel Van Camp, and Esq. Jenkins, who was familiar with the ground, all of whom are now dead.

The author of the R. R. Guide finds fault that the name of a Greek Sage, Seneca, has been applied to the Seneca Lake, which he says the Indians called Honeoye or Hemlock Lake—a strange confusion of names. Honeoye Lake is farther west than Seneca, and still retains its Indian name. The original name of the Seneca was Canadesaga Lake.

While complaining of the classic names he finds in the Lake country, he says it is refreshing to find such short aboriginal sounds as *Penn Yan*. This name, it is well known, is not of Indian derivation. The same writer locates Sullivan's Indian battle at *Elmira*, in front of the bridge, and speaks of the Indian embankment extending to the left as far as the high mountain *westward of the town*, and at *the base of which* Newtown Creek flows into the Chemung. It is at the base of the mountain *East* instead of West of the town where Newtown Creek flows to the River.

The tribe of Senecas have long been known by that appellation; and there is no doubt they are the same tribe spoken of by De Laet, who, in his journal of a voyage up the Hudson, speaks of "the right or eastern bank as inhabited by the Manhattaes or Manathanes, a cruel nation, and enemy of our people; while the left shore, he says, is possessed by the *Sanhikans*, mortal enemies of the others, a better and more civilized nation; they live along the rivers and bays in the midst of the country."

In the State Library in Albany, among the maps in the Warden collection is a map of *Nova Anglia*, by Joh. Baptista Homann, which represents "Senne-caas Lacus" extending E. & W. with Great Esopus River, running from the Erie to the Hudson.

The position of this lake is some 60 miles from *Esopus*.

Another old map, no date, places *Sene-ge* East of the Salt Spring.

In D'Auville's map of 1755, the Senecas are placed along the whole borders of the Lakes Ontario and Cayuga.

It is doubtless true that the Senecas are the same people called *Sennakins* in the ancient maps. The Lake defined as the Seneca on these old maps, may once have covered that extensive tract of wet land at the sources of the Esopus, Kill and Rondout Rivers called the "Drowned Lands."

The location of the battle ground has never been mistaken among the old settlers; all agree in fixing it at the same point as do all the soldiers who were in the Expedition. But there is an authority from one of the officers in Sullivan's Expedition, which should settle the question if it admitted of dispute.

Col. Proctor commanded the artillery in that expedition, and was in March 1791, sent by Gen. Washington in company with Capt. G. M. Houdon, a French officer of reputation, who also served in the Revolution, and Capt. Waterman Baldwin, on a mission to Corn-Planter's village. In his journal of that expedition, in my possession, I find the following note:

"Sunday March 27. Dined at Mr. Isaac Baldwin's and halted for the night and reviewed the ground on which the British and Indians were entrenched for better than a mile against the forces under Maj. Gen. Sullivan, Aug. '79. I also saw many traces made by our round and grape shot against them, and a large collection of pieces of 5 1-2 in. shells, which I formerly had the pleasure of causing to be exploded among them."

This pile of shells lay at the north-west corner of the old dwelling house of Col. Isaac Baldwin. And the writer well recollects having often seen them when a boy.

Many of the early settlers, John McHenry, John Fitz Simons, the two Baldwins, (above named) Daniel Van Campen and others, all unite in describing the scene of the battle-ground as here indicated, and they were engaged in the battle and could not be mistaken as to the locality.

The following note to one of the village papers may not be uninteresting as to the growth of the village since 1798:

Messrs. Editors—I observe in your paper of this morning that you state the census of the village of Elmira to be as follows:

1st Ward,	4,287
2d "	4,685
3d "	1,135
Total,	10,107

Curiosity induced me to compare this statement with an old document in my possession, being a "particular list or description of each dwelling house, &c., owned, possessed and occupied on the 1st day of October 1798, in the second sub-division, being within the 6th assessment District in the 9th Division in the State of New York," comprising the entire county of Tioga as it then existed. I copy the list of the buildings within the corporate limits of the present village of Elmira, to show the change since 1798, which may interest your readers:—

1. Guy Maxwell, at Newtown Point, on Water Street, frame house 32 by 23, valued at, ... $800 00
2. James Irwin, on Pine Street, Newtown Point, hewed logs 20 by 20, (the Master White House where Haight's Hotel now stands,) 150 00
3. Matthias Hollenback, on Water Street, 29 by 20, part logs and frame, ... 250 00
4. Amos Park, on Water Street, frame, 26 by 18, . . 350 00
5. Nicholas Gale, on Water Street, hewed logs and weatherboarded, 62 by 20. . . . . . 500 00
6. Christian Schott, on Main Street leading to the Court House adjoining the liberties of the Gaol, (now Sullivan) frame 28 by 20, ... 150 00
7. Lemuel Churchill, east side of Main, (now Sullivan) 18 by 16, square logs, ... 110 00
8. Nathan Teall, Main Street, leading to the Court House, 20 by 20, logs, ... 130 00
9. Joseph Hinchman, east of Union Street, adjoining Jail liberties, 30 by 30, frame, ... 400 00
10. Robt. Starrett, Water Street, (The Kline Tavern House,) 30 by 30, frame, ... 600 00
11. Maj. Swiney, Water Street, adjoining N. Gale, frame 28 by 20, ... 400 00
12. John Gregg, on Ferry Street, logs, 18 by 15, Distillery 20 by 24, ... 125 00
13. John McKenzie, Water Street, adjoining Jas. Brown, plank, 20 by 18, (Perry Lot) J. K. Perry, . . 200 00
14. Peter Masterton, Water Street, adjoining A. Park, frame, 30 by 24, ... 550 00
15. John Konkle, **Water Street, frame, 20 by 16,** . 300 00

16. John Stoner, east of Main, (now Sullivan) adjoining V. Matthews, 34 by 20, hewed logs, . . . 125 00
17. Peter Loop, east of Main, (now Sullivan-St.,) frame 22 by 18, ... 300 00
18. John Briggs, north of Second Street, adjoining J. Konkle, square logs, 36 by 18, ... 105 00
19. Jas. Brown, Water Street, adjoining McKenzie, logs, clap-boarded, 23 by 21, (where the residence of Stephen Tuttle now is,) 400 00
20. Cornelius Lowe, Water Street, logs 28 by 22, kitchen 18 by 22, (where Lyman Covell now resides,) . . 350 00
21. Dennis McLaughlin, log house, . . . 20 00
22. John Miller, house 34 by 17 . . . . 50 00
23. Selah Matthews, east side of Main, (now Sullivan) frame 20 by 16, ... 300 00

$6,665 00

To this should be added as now in the Third Ward :
24. John Sly, south side of the Tioga River, near the Ferry, at Newtown Point, frame 38 by 22. . . . 150 00

$6,815 00

I believe the only buildings in this list, now left, are the Konkle house, owned by the estate of James Benson, and perhaps a log house near where the old court house formerly stood.

ELMIRA, July 30, 1855. T. M.

The paper to which the above allusion is made is an Assessment Roll or Descriptive List of the houses, lots, etc., in the 6th Assessment District of the 9th Division of the State of New York, comprising the entire county of Tioga, and comprising the present counties of Broome, Chemung and Tioga, made under the Act levying a direct Tax, under the administration of the elder Adams, as they existed on the 1st October, 1798, made by Guy Maxwell, principal Assessor, aided by John Miller, John Konkle, Samuel Tinkham, Isaiah Sluyter, and George Harper, which shows the names of all the property holders in the now County of Chemung:

Vincent Mathews,	Daniel Sullivan,	Nathaniel Dunn,
James Irwin,	Henry Starrett,	Samuel Drake,
Guy Maxwell,	Benjamin Scoonoven,	John Durham,
John Sly,	Ebenezer Sayre,	George Gardner,
Joseph Miller,	James Sayre,	Asa Gildersleve,

David Griswold,
Jonas Bellows,
Caleb Fulkerson,
Amos Park,
Nicholas Gale,
Christian Scott,
Lemuel Churchill,
Nathan Teall,
Jos. Hinchman,
John Nicholson,
Wm Osborn,
Brinton Paine,
Amos Rowley,
Joel Rowley,
Ezra Rowley,
John Rickey,
Adam Sly,
Moses Depuy,
Thomas McClure,
Dennis McLaughlin,
John Miller,
Jacob Lowman,
Frederic Cassell,
William Wynkoop,
Johnson Miller,
Elijah Buck,
Daniel McDowell,
Joseph Bennett,
Enoch Warren,
Enoch Warren, Jr.,
Robt. Sarrett,
Thomas Baldwin,
Abram Middaugh,
Abram Miller,
Samuel Tubbs,
Elijah G. Wheeler,
John McHenry,
Roswell Goff,
Henry Shriver,
John Gregg,
John McKenzie,
Peter Masterton,

John Tenbrook,
David VanAuken,
Clark Winans,
Thomas Whitney,
Aaron Whitney,
John Winkler,
John W. Watkins,
Francis Sneckenbarger
David Bailey,
James Broderick,
James Bower,
John Brees,
John Cortright,
Joshua Carpenter,
Phineas Catlin,
Daniel Coryell,
Francis Conoway,
James H Wilson,
James Brown,
Cornelius Lowe,
Wilkes Jenkins,
Timothy Smith,
John Shepard,
Jacob Stoll,
Peter Barlow,
James Bailey,
Benjamin Bailey,
Jos. Drake,
Jno. Wilson,
Abel Pease,
John Vorse,
John Budd,
Jos. Benight,
Isaac Baldwin,
Henry Wells,
Gershom Bennett,
Josiah Hammond,
Benj. Drake,
John Dakin,
John Jennings,
Michael Sly,
Andrew McDowell,

John Hendy,
Samuel Hendy,
Stoddard Conkling,
Thomas Layton,
Harmon Lutkins,
Jacob Layre,
James Lounsbury,
James Latta,
Christian Minier,
Hugh Miller,
Daniel Middaugh,
Peter Mead,
Gershom Livesay,
John McConnell,
Mathew McConnell,
Joseph McConnell,
Samuel McConnell,
Abram Brewer,
Thomas Burt,
John Hillman,
Abiel Fry,
John Squires,
Benj. Burt,
Eben Green,
Abijah Batterson,
Israel Parshal,
Samuel Kress,
Christian Kress,
Samuel Westbrook,
Christian Hart,
Adam Hart,
Elijah Griswold,
Justus Bennett,
Gideon Griswold,
Iona Griswold,
David Burt,
Asahel Burnham,
Kinney Burnham,
Iona Rockwell,
Iona Rockwell, Jr,
Thaddeus Bennett,
Hamilton Tubbs,

John Konkle,	James Green,	Abner Kelsey,
Selah Matthews,	Enoch Kenyon,	George Charles,
John Stoner,	Peter Vandeventer,	James Mitchell,
Henry Baldwin,	John Green,	Wm. Jenkins,
Peter Loop,	Abner Wells,	John Mitchell,
John Briggs,	James Matthews,	Conrad Smith,
Jeremiah Hasbrouck,	Mathew Carpenter,	David Bennett,
Wm. VanGorder,	Daniel Cooley,	Josiah Reeder,
Samuel Middaugh,	Samuel Seely,	Gamaliel Townsend,
Lebeus Hammond,	Timothy Smith,	John Kinney,
Joshua Moss,	Caleb Seely,	Samuel Bydelman,
Solomon Bovier,	Caleb Smith,	Saml. VanGorder,
Green Bentley,	Caleb Baker,	John I. AcMoody,
Selah Matthews,	James Seely,	James Cameron,
Adam Seely,	Samuel Edsall,	Jacob Miller,
Israel Seely,	Samuel Tuthill,	John Bovier,
Abner Hetfield,	John Fitz Simins,	Thomas Hendy.
	John Smith,	

The first settlers of the Chemung and Susquehannah Valleys were composed of emigrants from Orange County, and the counties of Northampton in Pennsylvania, and Sussex in New Jersey, on either side of the Delaware River, together with many families who had originally settled near Wyoming, in Pennsylvania, under the Connecticut title, who had been driven from their settlements by the authorities of Pennsylvania, who asserted the prior and better claim of Wm. Penn to the territory in controversy, as they alleged. Those from the Delaware frontier had been engaged in controversies with the Indians in their irruptions into the frontier settlements during the Revolutionary War, and very many of them had accompanied the expedition of Gen. Sullivan into the Indian country in 1779, thus becoming acquainted with those rich valleys.

They were men of great energy, perseverance and far-seeing sagacity; there were no pigmies among them; they were stalwart men, and it might well be said, as of the men of old, "there were giants in those days." The settlements commenced in 1788, and the greater portion of the pioneers were here as early as 1790. Very few of us in this age of luxury and refinement can appreciate the toils and sufferings of these hardy pioneers, or what they gave up in leaving the old settlements from which they emigrated, surrounded by every earthly comfort, where schools were abundant, and the sound of the "church going bell" familiar to the ear, to face the privations to which they were subjected in forming a new settlement in a wilderness, inhabited by the wild beasts of the forest, or the more terrible red man of the woods.

Those who first located near Tioga Point, found no mill nearer than Wilkesbarre, a distance of ninety miles. To float down the Susquehannah in a canoe loaded with grain, and return with it after being ground, *poling up stream*, required about a week's labor. The active spirit of the American would not permit the wilderness to remain long unpeopled. The pride of a New Englander is to be a freeholder. The early marriages in the country led the younger to seek homes, and with the axe and the rifle on their shoulder, they sought them in the wilderness. The Indian clearings on the rivers soon enabled them to raise corn and potatoes in abundance. Fish, fowl and game of every kind were plentiful, and the first settlers were expert in their capture. The rifle was their greatest reliance in procuring provisions, as well as their protection against their savage neighbors. Good fellowship prevailed among them, and to see men going twenty or thirty miles to assist at the raising of a log house or barn, was an incident of frequent occurence. Universal kindness and hospitality prevailed and all comers were welcomed to the humble but abundant fare with which their tables were loaded. Selfishness had then no sway among men; every one was willing to share his substance with his neighbor, and was ready and willing to aid him in his pursuits,—and thus good offices went round. The man who was ready to help his neighbor was equally sure of aid when his necessities required it; the call was cheerfully made and as cheerfully responded to.

With the increase of population, however, these generous and noble impulses ceased, in some measure; but for a long time they were the peculiar characteristics of this contented and happy people. As the country became more densely populated and land became more valuable, selfishness began to creep in—controversies about division lines began to take place. The settlement of difficulties between neighbors, made by "leaving it out," as it was then termed, to one or two neighbors in whom each had confidence, became less prevalent. Lawyers began to come in—but fortunately, they were men of peace, and with the steady efforts of the influential citizens tended to prevent litigation, and the good old system of arbitration long maintained its ascendancy. School-houses began to be constructed and were well patronized; and houses of public worship, of a simple style of architecture, it is true, but sufficient for a humble and unpretending people, were scattered around, and filled with devoted worshippers.

It may well be doubted whether among the older settled portions of the country there could be found a race of men in every vocation and every profession, who were superior to these pioneers. In the profession of the law the old county of Tioga numbered the names of Vincent Matthews, John Wickham, Nathaniel W. Howell, David Jones, Peter Masterton, Mason Whiting, William Stuart, the two De Haerts of Binghamton, and many others whose talent would do credit to any country.

Among physicians, the names of Joseph Hinchman, Amos Park and Stephen Hopkins are well known and highly appreciated.— Among the settlers generally, a great amount of sound judgment, plain practical common sense and an astonishing degree of general information was conspicuous every where. Nor was the gentleman of the old school wanting among them. Very many names could be given who, for politeness, and the noble and true bearing of the finished gentleman, were unsurpassed in any quarter of the Republic. Their intelligence and sound sense is abundantly demonstrated in the fact of their selection of a country for a home, so rich in all the facilities for extensive internal improvement, and the impress of their sagacity remains in the rapid manner in which these great resources have been developed.

These hardy, self-sacrificing men have passed away. The soil once honored by their stately tread of conscious manhood, now covers all that was mortal of these fearless patriots. Their descendants may well boast of their virtues and feel their hearts beat at the recollection of their noble achievements. A few short years had only passed on their arrival here, since the Federal Constitution had received the assent of the American people, and the earliest settlers came in the same year. The hardy pioneers had rallied around it as the anchor of hope, with a determination to sustain it as the bond which was to unite the "Old Thirteen" in the brotherhood of love and union; and with an equal determination to frown down the man who should dare to raise a parricidal hand against it; when a doubt of its stability, or of the honesty and patriotism of the venerated men who united in its formation, was considered nothing less than High Treason against the common weal, and he who dared to express it would have found the neighborhood too hot for his comfort. It was the government of their choice, and they were determined to uphold it. If party lines began to be drawn, no one doubted the patriotism of his neighbor, and the public good alone was the object of all, though they may have differed as to the process of reaching and ensuring it. All were influenced by the absorbing object of advancing the public welfare. Scarcely half a dozen years had passed since the fearless men who had pledged "life, fortune and honor" to sustain the immortal Declaration of Independence, had fully redeemed their solemn pledge, and the thirteen Colonies had assumed their rightful place among the nations of the earth, as free and independent States, and with the assent of Great Britain.

A majority of the pioneers themselves had battled for the right, in the defence of home and fire-side, and had been distinguished for their bravery and sacrifices in the common cause. Then, there was no North, no South, no East, no West; but a band of brothers, everywhere, alive to the necessity of sustaining their infant institutions as the germ of a great nation, destined to spread over the entire continent, in which they firmly believed. In how short a period has their most sanguine expectations been realized. In that day, no man dared to sit down and calmly calculate the value of the Union. It was considered a fixed fact; and none entertained a doubt of its perpetuity. It was formed in the spirit of compromise, and with a full view of the various interests of the Confederacy, and with a design to protect them all. Such being its design, they had a right to expect its perpetuity, and to see the entire continent covered with teeming and happy millions, in a very short period. Their fathers, through a long series of years, had tested the capacity of man for self-government, having been left by the mother country to govern themselves. In no part of the globe could a population of the same number be found where human rights were better understood, or had been more thoroughly canvassed.

Had any one then ventured to doubt the stability of this Government, or the honesty and patriotism of its founders, he would soon have been served with a "notice to quit," by the hardy pioneers. Numerous instances can be cited by those yet living, where early settlers, who had disregarded their word of honor—had refused to redeem the plighted pledge—or been guilty of acts of glaring dishonesty in their transactions with their fellow men, received such a notice, coupled with a pledge that teams should be ready at the appointed day to aid in their removal. *Go they must, and go they did.* The man who refused to do right by his neighbor, was compelled to seek refuge elsewhere. "Be just, and fear not," was their motto. They lived up to it themselves, and forced its observance by others. How much more then would such an offence against the common weal, as they deemed the doubting of the justice and wisdom of the common Union and the Constitution, have required the notice, and compelled the observance of its terms. One only instance, it is said ever occurred, and the individual endured for years the frowns of his fellows, and nothing was ever permitted to atone for the offence. It is gratifying to look back upon this primitive community, and to dwell upon their simple and rigid virtues.

Their wants were few, and were readily supplied in the abundance of the country. No one need want if possessed of a modicum of industry. In their transactions with each other they were rigidly guided by the Golden Rule, " Do unto others as you would that they should do unto you." And this too, without the intervention of lawyers, magistrates, or courts, who, as yet, had found no place among them.

Their dependence upon each other induced and perpetuated kindly feelings, and in such a community but few causes of controversy would arise. Neighborhood difficulties, if irreconcilable by the parties, were submitted at once to the arbitrament of discreet persons in whom the whole community had confidence—and there were hosts of such men among them—whose decision was final and without appeal. In a community where so much common sense prevailed, dissatisfaction seldom ensued, and the awards were quietly submitted to.

"Asking nothing but what was right, and submitting to nothing which was wrong," the protest against wrong made on the threshold, without waiting for a repetition of the offence, the community soon settled every controversy in accordance with that strong vein of common sense which so remarkably characterized these early settlers. Ideas of justice and equity prevailed everywhere; a violation of them in one instance was made the business of all, as all felt the same interest in having them carried out and sustained, lest they themselves might be the next victims. The English common law was as well understood here as in any part of the continent, and there were plenty of intelligent, strong-minded and determined men to advise and direct in every emergency.

Tedious litigation was then unknown and not permitted. Occasional resorts to fisty-cuffs took place. Fair play governed in every instance, and there were plenty to enforce and require it. The universal manliness compelled the vanquished to acknowledge the prowess of the victor, and, the battle over, they drank in friendship, and it was rare indeed that the controversy was renewed. Once settled, in either way, it was settled forever.

The Bible, the Declaration of Independence, Poor Richard's Almanac, and later, Washington's Farewell Address, composed the family library. These lights, and their desire to do justice, coupled with their generous and friendly dispositions, enabled them to exhibit the spectacle of a contented and happy people.

The County of Tioga was organized by the Legislature of 1791. It was taken out of territory previously embraced within the limits of Montgomery, which bore the name previous to, and during the war of the Revolution, and until the year 1784, of Tryon County—in honor of one of the English Colonial Governors, who unfortunately, proved himself during our National struggle, the uncompromising enemy of the American cause. The name had become so odious to the people of the State that, by Legislative enactment in that year, (1784,) it was changed to Montgomery, in honor of the Irish soldier and patriot, who fell at an early period of the war of Independence, in the gallant attack on Quebec, while leading his troops on that occasion—the 31st December, 1775.

At the date of the organization, it embraced its present limits and the Counties of Chemung, Broome, and Chenango. It was bounded by Otsego on the East, the Military Tract and Herkimer on the North, Ontario on the West, (from which Steuben was taken in 1796,) and by Pennsylvania on the South.

Its Towns, commencing at its westerly limits, were, Newtown, Chemung, Owego, (none of whose territory was where it is now, all of it lying west of the Owego Creek, and then embraced what is now Tioga,) Spencer, (except that part of it lying west of Cayuta Creek,) Barton and Nichols, in Tioga County, and Caroline, Danby, and Newfield, in Tompkins.

The town next easterly of Owego Creek was Union, which then included within its limits what is now known as Owego, Newark, Berkshire and Richford in Tioga, and the territory now known, as Union, Vestal, Lisle, &c., in Broome, and the westerly portion of what is now Chenango County. The town next east of Owego was Chenango; the next, easterly and northerly, was Jericho, which covered territory then lying in the easterly part of Chenango County as now located.

Thus it is seen, that the six old towns of Chemung, Owego, Union, Chenango and Jericho, then included territory which the fifty-two towns of Chemung, Tioga, Broome and Chenango counties and the three towns of Caroline, Danby and Newfield in Tompkins now cover, numbering in all fifty-five.

The first loss of territory which old Tioga sustained in the organization of other counties was in 1798, when the northeasterly corner of her ancient domain, and a strip from the westerly part of Herkimer, were taken to form the County of Chenango then erected;

which in its turn was found large enough, in 1806 to admit, Madison to be taken from its northern half. Next, in order of time, 1806, was the organization of Broome County taken from Tioga, and so named in honor of their Lieut. Governor, John Broome. It embraced when first organized, the old towns of Chenango, &c., and territory now called Newark, Owego, Berkshire and Richford in Tioga.

The next change in the boundaries of Tioga County took place in 1823, the year subsequent to the burning of the court-house at Spencer Village; at which time the territory now included within the four towns of Owego, Newark, Berkshire and Richford, was taken from Broome and restored to Tioga, and the then town of Danby, Caroline and Newfield before that date comprised within Tioga, were annexed to Tompkins. At the same time Tioga was divided into two jury districts, Owego and Elmira becoming the half shires, in each of which a new court-house was erected. This was the preliminary step to the establishment of Chemung, which was doubtless then contemplated, and resulted in 1834, in a complete severance of the connection and mutuality of interests which since 1791 had bound the territory comprised within the present limits by that flourishing county to the ancient name and honors of Tioga. After a union of forty-five years the final separation took place, and a new geographical line since then has been interposed between them, an imaginary barrier however, as it has since 1798, been between Tioga, the mother, and Chenango, Broome, and the three towns in Tompkins, the daughters. The old settlers in Chemung, as now organized, struggled manfully for the cherished name of Tioga, endeared to them by a thousand fond recollections, and the still stronger one as they claimed, that the river Tioga from which the ancient name of the county arose, still remained in the boundaries of Chemung, and none of it in the newly formed county of Tioga. They thought and claimed that they should retain the old name, while the other should have more appropriately been named Susquehanna, as that majestic river passes through the entire territory. It is true that the river after its junction with the Cohocton at Painted Post, is now called Chemung, but anciently it was called Tioga its whole length and to its junction with the Susquehanna at Tioga Point, now Athens, in Pennsylvania.

In the minds of the surviving pioneers and their descendants, however, no modern lines of demarkation can separate their pioneer fame, nor obliterate cherished memorials or ancient landmarks upon the page of truthful history; their wondrous story will ever be found united and indivisible, as certainly and as naturally as the waters which sweep the vallies of the Chemung and Susquehanna unite in one volume. Tioga Point—the name Tioga, or *Ta-ya-o-gah*, as the Indians pronounced it, means the forks, or a point formed by the junction of streams, or perhaps more poetically " the meeting of the waters." Its very name indicates a point, so that the addition of "Point," made by the early settlers was tautology and probably originated in their ignorance of the Indian language. It was a favorite addition to many localities, and like the Indian names, was descriptive of the locality—as Chenango Point, Tioga Point, Olean Point, &c.

From the date of the first infant effort at internal improvement, commencing with the issue of the first commission in 1797, to Phineas Catlin and Mathew Carpenter, (the latter of whom was succeeded by John Hendy) "to lay out the road leading from Catskill Landing, upon the Hudson, to Catharinestown in the County of Tioga," to the projection and completion of the New York & Erie Rail Road, through "the Southern Tier,"—that crowning triumph of this triumphal era—the pioneer struggles, and patriotic efforts of their inhabitants have been encouraged and strengthened by a sympathetic and heartfelt mutuality. Their hopes and fears have been in unison; their defeats and victories shared in the kindest brotherhood—co-equals in public spirit, and in its substantial and enduring rewards.*

Chemung County being taken from Tioga by Act of 29th March, 1836, dividing the old County by a line beginning on the east bank of the Chemung river, on the Pennsylvania line; thence up the river by its banks, at low water mark to a Sulphur Spring near the center of the lower Narrows; thence in a direct line north-east to the south-east corner of Lot No. 153; thence north along the south line of Lots 153, 201, 202 and 203, to the south line of the town of Erin; thence by such line to the Cayuta Creek; thence up the center of said creek to the south line of the town of Cayuta; thence east by that line to the east line of Cayuta; thence north by such line to the line of the county of Tompkins.

All that part lying west of this line now forms the County of Chemung. The Act erecting the County of Schuyler, took from the boundaries of Chemung two of her towns, Catharine and Dix, and part of Cayuta, leaving the remainder, to which the name of Van Etten was applied, still in Chemung.

Big Flatts was taken from Elmira April 16, 1822.

Catlin taken from Catharine, April 16, 1823.

---

* The Compiler has availed himself of many of the statistics given by Judge AVERY in his sketches of the Susquehannah Valley.

Cayuta taken from Spencer 30th March 1824, part now in Schuyler, remained in Chemung by the name of Van Etten.

Chemung organized February 16, 1791.

Elmira taken from Chemung by name of Newtown, April 10, 1792, changed to Elmira in 1811.

Erin taken from Chemung, March 1822.

Southport taken from Elmira April 16, 1822.

Veteran taken from Catharine 16th April, 1823.

Horseheads taken from Elmira, act of 1854.

THE PIONEERS' PLEA FOR OLD TIMES.

WRITTEN FOR THE PIONEERS' HISTORICAL FESTIVAL AT OWEGO, FEBRUARY 22, 1855.

BY C. L. WARD, ESQ., OF TOWANDA, PA.

We'll wake a plain old fashioned muse
Upon this festal day,
And sing of scenes and talk of times
Which long since passed away:
As thus we've met, 't is well to take
A retrospective view,
And note what changes have been wrought
Since this, our land, was new.

Then—all agreed, without dispute,
To call Ohio "West";
And did not dream of world's beyond,
But were content to rest
Amid these smiling vales of ours,
Where sugar-maple grew.
So here we reared our forest homes,
When this our land was new.

Ours was a brave and gallant band,
Well fitted for each toil,
And soon we let the sunbeams in
Upon a generous soil ;
Strong were the hands, and strong the hearts,
Of that widely-gathered few,
Who conquered here, old forests grand,
When this our land was new.

Dark danger lurked around each cot,
The red men in their wrath
Lay coiled like silent serpents,
Along each greenwood path ;
Or shouted loud their battle-cry,
As over hill and glen they flew—
Ah! those were "times that tried men's souls!"
When this our land was new.

The gaunt wolf's howl and panther's scream,
Made hideous every night,
And wives and youthful maiden's hearts
Oft trembled with affright;
Until at length they learned to share
That courage stern and true,
Which throbbed in every manly breast,
When this our land was new.

War's storm swept past, and gentle peace
With silent blessings comes,
And fills with hopes and gladness
Our wood embosomed homes ;
And neighbor, then, toward neighbor
In friendship closely drew,
So we lived a band of brothers,
When this our land was new.

No party feuds, or politics,
Much marred our rural joys,
One hope engrossed each female heart,
And nerved the men and boys.
To clear a farm—adorn a home—
Was most they had in view.
We'd no foreign frips or fopperies,
When this our land was new.

The girls all learned to make good bread,
While like their spinning-wheels,
Right merry ran their sinless songs,
Without piano peals.
And blithely did they dance at night,
E'en when they staid till two—
Such were the *only stays* they wrought,
When this our land was new.

Most wore a linsey-woolsey dress,
Their own sweet hands had made,
With a blue and white checked apron
That would not tear or fade;
The rich brocades and rustling silks,
Were seldom brought to view,
Except " to go to meetin' " in,
When this our land was new.

Five yards were ample for a dress,
Few ever asked for more,
And never trailed their skirts along
The dirty streets or floor.
They looked as neat and tidy then,
As any one of you
Who scorn the homespun, which was worn
When this our land was new.

We seldom saw consumption then,
With its pallor and its pall,
'T was rounded cheeks, and Health's own bloom,
That greeted every call.
Each foot a home-knit stocking wore,
A home-made calfskin shoe,
And there's certain things—girls did n't wear,
When this our land was new.

Good, wholesome and substantial food,
Our festive tables crowned ;
No French nick-nack or luxury,
In our bills of fare was found ;
But labor sweetned every dish,
And what is better too,
We needed no " Maine Liquor Law "
When this our land was new.

Yes! things *have* changed, there's little left
Of plain old-fashioned truth,
All dream of princely riches now,
E'en from their very youth;
And Schuyler shifts, and scoundrel schemes,
Rise frequently to view,
And make us mourn those pure "old times"
When this our land was new.

To half the folks Ohio's *East!*
Missouri's at the best,
A kind of half-way resting place
To those who're going West.
Pacific States were all the rage
Until the late ado,
Now Kansas or Nebraska is
The only land that's new.

Millions are blest and blessing now,
Where sixty years agone,
The poor untutored Indian roamed
A monarch, and alone;
The iron-horse with fire and fright,
Whirls quick the country through,
Where we wagged "many a weary foot"
When this our land was new.

Our women no more spin and weave,
In which we're all agreed,
With patent rights and power-looms
There is no longer need;
But then for bread they give us *Stone*,
Or do us *Brown* or blue,
They did not then put *Bloomers* on,
When this our land was new.

But enough of retrospection,
And the changes which have come,
To each and all around us,
Bringing joy or bringing gloom;
And, let's raise our thoughts in sadness,
Before we say adieu!
In memory of our loved and lost
Since this our land was new.

The Whitneys, Platts, and Robinsons,
Pumpellys, Averys, Gores,
The Franklins, Maxwells, Spaldings,
The Welles and the Moores,
The Satterlees and Hollenbacks,
Rosses and Tuttles too,
Who blessed with dauntless energies
This land, when it was new.

God rest them! in their last low homes,
With all their brave compeers,
Who fought and bled, or toiled and strove,
Through weary, lingering years,
That thus their sons, in prosperous peace,
Could pleasantly review
The many changes time has wrought,
Since this our land was new.

GUY MAXWELL, one of the proprietors of DeWittsburgh, was born in Ireland, July 15, 1770. His parents left a port in Scotland for America, in June 1770, and were shipwrecked in the Irish Channel, and were thrown on the shores of the County of Down, where he was born soon after. In 1772, the family made a second attempt, and reached the American shores at Annapolis, in Maryland, and made a settlement at Martinsburgh, Va., near the Potomac. Their son, Guy, was placed in the store of Gen. James O'Hara, then of Martinsburgh, afterwards of Pittsburgh, Pa., to "learn the art, trade and mystery of a merchant." His term expired at the age of eighteen, on the 15th July, 1788. He was to have accompanied Gen. O'Hara to Pittsburgh, but the arrival of Col. Hollenback, of Wilkesbarre, on a visit to his Virginia relatives, at the time, changed his destination, and he accompanied him on his return to Wilkesbarre; and in Sept. 1788, commenced business with Col. Hollenback at Tioga Point, (now Athens,) and remained there until August 1796, when he removed to Elmira, to engage in the mercantile business and superintend the sale of his village plot. He was soon after appointed Sheriff of Tioga, by Gov. George Clinton, which office he held for a number of years, and also held other positions of trust and profit. He died February 23d, 1814, at less than forty-four. He had been concerned with the late Stephen Tuttle in building a flouring mill on Newtown Creek, and in mercantile business in the village, in connection with the late Thomas M. Perry, under the firm of Perry & Co., which closed about the year 1808.

Mr. TUTTLE settled in Elmira in 1818, and died a few years since universally esteemed. His wife survived him about ten years, and died at the age of eighty-seven. They could say with the celebrated Logan—that no one ever left their roof hungry or in want.

WILLIAM HOFFMAN came to Elmira from Northumberland, Pa., in 1799, with his worldly goods in a pocket-hankerchief. He engaged in the Hatting business, but left it to become a model farmer, and still survives, an honorable specimen of the early pioneer, enjoying a green old age, surrounded by all that can render a man comfortable, with hosts of friends, who love and respect him.

HENRY WISNER, the proprietor of the westerly portion of the village, was a resident of Warwick, in the county of Orange. He was a member of the Continental Congress, and voted for Independence on the 2d July 1776, but the next day (as appears by the journals of that body,) was called home to take command of his regiment in the field; and left before the declaration was engrossed, and his name does not appear to that imperishible document. His liberality in the gift of a public square, and other lands to the citizens of Elmira, are an honorable monument to his memory. There are many other individuals whose names should appear in a full history of the first settlement of the country, which may yet appear, but the limited space devoted to this publication prevents it.

The treaty held at Elmira with the Six Nations, by Col. Pickering on the part of the United States, took place in 1791. A previous one was held at Tioga Point in 1790, commencing on the 16th and closing on the 23d November. The tribes there represented, were the Oneidas, Onondagas, Cayugas, Chippewas and Stockbridge Indians. The difficulty which called the Council together, was amicably arranged by the shrewdness of Pickering, who then resided at Wilkesbarre. Hendrick Appaumut, an eloquent Stockbridge, Red Jacket, Corn-Planter, Farmer's Brother, Little Billey, and Fish-Carrier, an able and distinguished warrior of the Cayugas, were present.— They came to the council excited; but Pickering had quieted them, and at the close, Red Jacket delivered an inflammatory speech in reference to the sale of their lands to Phelps & Gorham, at the treaty of Fort Stanwix in October 1784. To enquire into the charges of

Fraud at that treaty, a meeting was appointed to be held at Painted Post on the 17th June, 1791; but the papers in reference to it show that it was held at Newtown, though called the Treaty of Painted Post. There are yet persons living who were present and well recollect the circumstances. The Indians, according to the statement of Capt. Geo. Gardner, encamped in the westerly part of the village, and their tents were ranged from where the Brainard House now stands to the upper part of the village. The conferences were held a part of the time under the Council Tree on the flat east of the court-house, on the premises now owned by Hector M. Seward, Esq., who religiously protects the spot where the old tree stood, and were completed on the flats where the State Fair was held on the grounds of Mrs. Arnot. Among the papers in reference to this treaty, which are preserved, it appears that a copy of the Release from the Six Nations to Phelps & Gorham, was presented by Col. Pickering, and a certificate signed by him, dated at Newtown Point in the State of New York, July 7, 1791, states that he had shown the Release to Fish-Carrier and other Chiefs then present, who stated the terms of the Release to be the same as the one then presented; and another signed by Pickering, dated at Newtown, in the State of New York, July 16, 1791, states that the day before "the principal Sachems of the Senecas now attending the Treaty held by me with the Six Nations at this place," assured him that they were satisfied with the Treaty of Fort Stanwix, and that Red Jacket and Corn-Planter understood it as they did at the time, and that the statements made by them at Tioga Point in Nov. 1790, were unfounded and mischievously intended.

There is also the examination of Col. Matthias Hollenback, who was present at the treaty of Fort Stanwix and also at Newtown, taken before Brinton Paine, one of the judges of Tioga County, at Newtown Point on the 14th of July, 1791, showing the fallacy of these complaints—also the deposition of Thomas Rees, of Northumberland, taken at the same time, and those of Elisha Lee and Eleazer Lindley, on the 5th of May, 1791, and a statement of the allegations made before Pickering, by Red Jacket, at Tioga Point on the 21st of November, 1790. The investigation terminated in a satisfactory manner.

The visit of Louis Phillippe, late King of France, and his two brothers at Elmira, in 1797, is a notable event. He had spent some time in Switzerland as a teacher and afterwards served in the French army as an aid-de-camp to a French General, under the assumed name of Corby, until 1794. Suspicions were excited as to his true character and he left the army and the country and remained some time in Denmark. His father had perished on the scaffold and his mother had been imprisoned in Paris, and his two brothers, the Duc de Montpensier, and the Count de Beaujolais, had been shut up in the Castle of St. Jean at Marseilles.

In 1796 communication had been opened between the Dutchess of Orleans (their mother,) and the French Directory, and she was informed that if she would induce her elder son, the Duc d' Orleans to repair to the United States, the sequestration should be removed from her property and her two younger sons should be released and permitted to join their brother in America.

Under this arrangement, the King set sail from Hamburg for the United States, in the ship America, Captain Ewing of Philadelphia on the 24th of September, 1796, and arrived in Philadelphia twenty-seven days thereafter.

The other brothers sailed from Marseilles and arrived in Philadelphia after a tedious passage of ninety-three days. After the union of the brothers they spent the winter in Philadelphia, mingling in the first society there. They visited General Washington, at Mount Vernon, and travelled through Virginia, Kentucky and parts of Ohio, and early in June arrived at Buffalo.

On their way from Buffalo to Canandaigua, then almost in a state of nature, they met Alexander Baring, (afterwards Lord Ashburton) whom the King had seen at Philadelphia, where he married a daughter of Wm. Bingham. After a few minutes conversation they pursued their respective routes, Mr. Baring telling the King, (as General Cass relates,) "that he had left an almost impassable road behind him, and the King answering by the comfortable assurance, that Mr. Baring, would find no better one before him." The brothers soon after arrived at Canandaigua, where they spent some weeks, under the hospitable roof of Thomas Morris, then a resident there. They continued their route to Geneva, where they procured a boat and embarked on the Seneca Lake, which they ascended to its head. Here they remained a few days at the house of Mr. George Mills, and shouldering their packs, came on to Elmira on foot, bringing letters from Mr. Morris to Henry Towar and other residents of the place. It was a wonderful mutation in human affairs, that he who entered our village with a pack on his back should so soon have occupied a Throne. Here they remained about ten days, boarding at the Tavern kept by Mrs. Seely, the widow of Nathaniel Seely (afterwards called the Kline House.) Mr. Towar furnished them with a Durham boat, well fitted up, in which they descended the Chemung, and

Susquehanna rivers to Wilksbarre, from whence they proceeded across the country to Philadelphia. In a letter, dated at Philadelphia, August 14th, 1797, from the Duc de Montpensier to his sister, the Princess Adelaide of Orleans, describing their journey, he says " It took us four months—we travelled during that time, a thousand leagues, and always upon the same horses, except the last 100 leagues, which we performed partly by water, partly on foot, partly on hired horses, and partly in the stage, or public conveyance. We have seen many Indians, and remained several days in their country. To give you an idea of the agreeable manner, in which they travel in this country, I will tell you that we passed fourteen nights, in the woods, devoured by all kinds of insects, after being wet to the bone, without being able to dry ourselves, and eating pork and sometimes a little salt beef and corn bread." The work of General Cass, entitled " France, its King and People," gives many interesting details of this visit of the French King.

An examination of the Assessment Roll of 1798, so often referred to, will show some singular facts as to the increased value of real estate in and about Elmira, in sixty years. The best farms of the Chemung valley, the Hammond farm, the Miller farm, the McDowell flats, the Jenkins farm, the Sly farms, are assessed in that year at $10 per acre, the others on Seely Creek and the plains about Elmira and towards Horseheads and Big Flatts at from five to eight dollars per acre. The Starret farm, the heart of Big Flatts, at ten dollars per acre—now not an acre of those lands can be purchased at less than sixty to one hundred dollars per acre, and many of them higher. The lots in Elmira previous to 1800 were sold at one to two hundred dollars for lots 100 feet front by 219 deep—now many of those lots bring from forty to one hundred dollars *per foot* front. The opening of the canals connected with the Erie Canal, gave the first impetus, to improvement. The completion of the New York & Erie Rail Road, with the energy and perseverance of those who have settled among us, and the wonderful power of steam have advanced half a century, the most sanguine expectations of the few persons (deemed half crazy for their predictions at the time,) who had ventured to prophecy the astonishing increase, which has since been attained. He who thirty years ago should have predicted the wonderful feats of the Electric Telegraph, would probably have been placed in a strait jacket; nor would he who should have prophesied in 1836 that the journey to New York could be performed with ease and comfort in ten or twelve hours, (except in a balloon) have fared much better. Yet we have lived to see Elmira, which thirty years ago numbered but her hundreds, *and every one well known*, now roll up her ten or twelve thousand, and many of us, scarcely know our next neighbor. The progress of the surrounding villages shows a similar state of things, and we already begin to talk of the cities of the Southern Tier, where a few years since, scarce a hamlet existed. In view of the past, and its astonishing results, what may we not expect of the future? The vast results produced by the spirit of the age aided by the wonderful power of steam and electricity, may well encourage us in the hope of still greater attainments. The opening of new canals and railroads, chequering the country in every direction, assisted by some new agent of power, which may yet be found to supersede the use of steam, may justly astound the few old settlers, who yet remain, and who have lived to see their fond hopes, and far reaching calculations realized long before the periods which they may have assigned for their consummation. That they did predict such results is a high compliment to their judgment and foresight.

The Masonic Fraternity of Elmira, has been so long established (nearly seventy years,) that it would seem that some notice should be taken of their institution in these sketches. It is known, that a traveling Lodge of Free Masons, accompanied Sullivan's Expedition and a Masonic funeral took place at Tioga Point, August 18th, 1779, in honor of Lieut. Jones and Capt. Davis who were buried at Pittston with Masonic honors, under a general order of the Commander-in-Chief, dated August 17th, 1779. Union Lodge No. 30 was instituted on the 26th of August, 1793, of which Amos Park was the First Master. He was re-elected for four terms, John Konkle two terms, Joseph Hinchman three terms, John Miller five terms, Caleb Baker four terms, Samuel Tuthill five terms, Elias Satterlee, who died while Master, John Cherry twice, George Guest, John Fitz Simmons, Orange Chapman, Daniel E. Brown twice, Isaac Roe, and Wyatt Carr to the time of its close, in 1827. Under its new organization, in 1843, B. B. Payne four times, James S. French five times, D. S. Hamilton twice, and William M. Gregg down to 1853, when the Sixtieth Anniversary of their organization was celebrated. At that time these statistics were collected. The following list of the departed members was then furnished, adding such as have died since:—

Horace Agard,	Abner Hetfield,	Nathaniel Seely,
Eben Bartlett,	Joseph Hinchman,	James Seely,
Caleb Baker,	Nathaniel Hinchman,	Berzaleel Seely,
Thomas Baldwin,	George Hornell,	John B. Seely,
William Baldwin.	Jared Hoyt,	Jonas Seely,

Isaac Baldwin,
Waterman Baldwin,
Ichabod Baldwin,
Isaac Baldwin, 2d,
Thomas Baldwin, Jr.,
Grant B. Baldwin,
Howell Bull,
David Bardslee,
Samuel Besley,
Seneca Baker,
John H. Brown,
A. A. Beckwith,
Jefferson Bartlett,
Platt Bennett,
Dugald Cameron,
Daniel Cruger,
James Cameron,
Phineas Catlin,
John Coe,
George Coryell,
Samuel Colegrove,
John Cherry,
Francis Collingwood,
Orange Chapman,
William Dunn,
Joseph Draper,
Eleazer Dana,
Jonathan Eaton,
Samuel Edsall,
John Fitz Simmons,
Jacob Gilbert,
Joseph Gillett,
William S. Garrad,
George Gardner,
Caleb L. Gardner,

E. S. Hinman,
Samuel Hendy,
John Hughes,
James Irwin,
Elijah Jones,
Ithamer Judson,
Samuel Ingals,
John Konkle,
Abner Kelsey,
Joseph Kingsbury,
Rev. John Kline,
John H. Knapp,
Nathaniel Knapp,
Aaron Konkle,
George Mills,
Noah Murray,
Ezekiel Mulford,
Vincent Mathews,
John Miller,
Peter Masterton,
John McCann,
George McClure,
H. M. Graves,
Charles Maxwell,
D. Cameron Maxwell,
O. O'Hanlon,
Amos Park,
Moses Park,
David Paine,
Michael Pfautz,
Jotham Purdy,
Samuel Ransom,
George Reeder,
Stephen Reeder,
William B. Rochester,

Samuel S. Seely,
John Stoner,
John Spalding,
Simon Spalding,
Wm. Spalding,
John Shepard,
Henry Shriver,
Christian Scott,
Joseph Smith,
Solomon L. Smith,
Abraham Shoemaker,
Robert D. Shappee,
Elias Satterlee,
Timothy S. Satterlee,
Charles Sherwood,
Whittington Sayre,
John S. Suffern,
Uriah Stevens,
John Stephens.
Ira Stephens,
John Spicer, 1821,
Nathan Teall,
Henry Towar,
Samuel Tuthill,
Stephen Tuttle,
George Townsend,
Fitch Wattles,
Walter Watrous,
John W. Watkins,
Clark Winans, Jr.,
Jacob Westlake,
John W. Wisner,
Isaac S. Wood,
Samuel Winton,
Isaac Roe,

Of the surviving members of the first organization, yet living are:—

A. S. Atkins, 1814,
Thomas Maxwell, 1814,
M. McReynolds, 1815,
H. W. Atkins, 1815,

G. H. Bull, 1817,
R. Bancroft, 1818,
L. Biles, 1818,
L. Hudson, 1818,

C. W. Dunn, 1819,
John Jackson, 1822,
Abraham Riker, 1822,
D. Bently, 1822,

W. Carr, 1823,   John C. Roe, 1826,   R. Hetfield, 1828,
C. Greatsinger, 1823, Samuel Riker, 1826,   Isaac Reynolds.
V. Conkling, 1826,

A new Lodge called Ivy Lodge has been established a few years, and both are flourishing, but the data to show their numbers since 1853 are not now at hand. In looking over the list of deceased members of the fraternity, particularly among the earlier ones, it is perceived that more than twenty of them bore arms in the war of the Revolution.

The ancient Indian name of the present village of Elmira was Ski-ne-do-wa, meaning "at the Great Plains." Subsequently it was named Ka-na-we-ola, meaning a "head on a pole." The tradition derived from Red Jacket in reference to this name is that about 1730 a council of the five nations was held here, at which one of their Chiefs was tried for some crime, convicted, be-headed and his head placed on a pole, a little west (as he said) from the old Council Tree, which would be where the present Court House now stands.

The County Seat is located at Elmira. The Court House and Jail and Clerk's Office are on Lake Street. The Chemung Canal extends South from Seneca Lake, through the central valley to the Chemung River at Elmira, forming a direct communication with the great chain of internal water navigation of the State. A navigable feeder from Corning, Steuben County, forms a junction with the Canal on the summit level at Horseheads. The Junction Canal extends several miles along the Chemung, affording navigation at points where the river is obstructed by rapids and narrows. The New York & Erie Rail Road extends along the Chemung River, through Chemung, Southport, Elmira and Big Flatts. The Chemung Rail Road extends North from Elmira, through Horseheads and Veteran to the Lake and Canandaigua. The Elmira & Williamsport Rail Road extends from Elmira, South, through Southport into Pennsylvania, forming a direct line to Philadelphia, Baltimore and Washington.

The first settlers, ranked among their numbers many men who had been actively engaged in the revolutionary war. Colonel John Hendy, who settled here in 1788, held a commission in a regiment of Northampton (Pennsylvania) troops, was engaged in the battles of Monmouth, Trenton and Princeton, and at the latter battle brought off from the battle field the body of General Mercer, a distinguished Virginia officer, who was wounded in that engagement and died subsequently of his wounds. He was a native of Northampton County,

Pennsylvania, where he was born September 3d, 1757; he held many town offices, and died in 1840, aged eighty-three years and upwards.

Brinton Paine, a Colonel of the State troops and a prisoner of war, in a British prison ship, died at the age of eighty-one. Mathew Carpenter, who bore arms in the same contest, died in 1839, at the age of eighty-one years. Selah Matthews, another of the soldiers of the Revolution, died in 1833, at seventy-one, and John Konkle, Esq., who served in New Jersey, and the first Postmaster of Elmira, aged seventy-three years.

These venerable relics of the stiring times of the American Revolution, were permitted to linger among us, as if by a special providence, that all of us might see and know the fearless patriots, who battled for the rights of freemen against such fearful odds, and to leave their example among us, to induce those who followed them to transmit to their children unimpaired, the inheritance, which by their valor and energy, had been thus secured to us. The truth of this will be exhibited to any one who visits the Cemeteries of Elmira, while he sees the names of many who were active in forwarding the public interest, who were laid there at forty and fifty years of age.

ELMIRA FEMALE COLLEGE.

Elmira has the honor of establishing the first regularly Chartered College for young ladies in the State of New York. There are now two others—the Ingham University and Vassar Female College, but both of these received their Charters at a more recent date.

The founding of the Elmira Female College grew out of the labors of Rev. Harvey A. Sackett and his wife, Mrs. D. H. Sackett, who began their efforts in the city of Auburn. A Charter with the beginning of a subscription was obtained, but owing to some discouraging circumstances, in the prosecution of the enterprize at Auburn, a proposition was laid before some of the citizens of Elmira, to transfer the institution to this place. This proposition was met in such a liberal manner, that the Charter was amended and the transfer took place. The name of the institution was then " The Elmira Collegiate Seminary"—with only the rank of a first class academy. Subsequently the Charter was so amended as to grant full Collegiate privileges and powers, of the same rank with the other Colleges of the State. A splendid College building was erected scarcely surpassed by any edifice of the kind in this country, chiefly after the designs of ——— Barker, Esq., of Westfield, N. Y., as Architect.

The College was dedicated in September, 1855, and in the following month was opened for students. For the first year, it was under charge of Mrs. M. A. W. Dunlap, as Vice President.

At the close of the first year, Rev. A. W. Cowles was elected and inaugurated as the first President, who still holds that office. The College has achieved a wide and growing reputation, so that probably no institution in this country occupies a higher place in respect to its extensive and thorough course of study — the actual success of the Faculty in the government and general management of the College, and in the marked results of able instruction in the high grade of scholarship which those have attained who have pursued the regular course of study. The enterprise has been a most decided success. Under the generous benefactions and financial skill of Simeon Benjamin, Esq., the College has reached a firm and permanent basis. Its property, as reported to the Regents of the University, amounts to more than $80,000. The income from term bills has been as high as $19,000 per annum, and has rarely been less than fifteen thousand.

Still, the College is but partially supplied with those things needful for its best growth and usefulness. The grounds need to be laid out as an ornament to the village. The building needs internal improvements, both in conveniences and in suitable decorations, such as frescoing the Chapel, fitting up the Halls, furnishing a Gymnasium, a Library, and such various additions and improvements as shall correspond with the high rank the College has attained, and with the reasonable expectations which are entertained by the friends of Education in this and other States.

A few thousand dollars for these purposes are now very much needed, and it would seem highly proper and reasonable that Elmira should make the College a beautiful and lasting ornament, as it is already an honor to the public spirit and liberality of the village, and to this section of the State.

The College is a constant means of extending the reputation of the village. Circulars, to the amount of two thousand a year, are scattered throughout the whole country, from Maine to California. Students from all the Northern States have been members of the College, and their friends and neighbors, and circles of correspondence, are made acquainted with Elmira and the College to which its name is attached.

Thus Elmira owes much of its present reputation and prosperity to this, among other sources and means of improvement.

ELMIRA WATER-CURE.

Under charge of S. O. Gleason. M. D., located on East Hill, built in 1852, by Fox Holden, M. Hale and S. O. Gleason, who still retain the ownership—Dr. Gleason having the entire charge of conducting it. Main building is 34x78, four stories; two wings, each 20x32, three stories high. Another building 36x20, two-and-a-half stories; eight acres in the lot; cost $15,000; can accommodate one hundred persons; water from a spring, conducted into the buildings through wooden pipes.

The beauty of its location is unsurpassed by any similar institution. Dr. Gleason has had thirty years experience in his profession. Mrs. Gleason has charge of the female patients, and is a regularly educated physician. The glens, hills, and wild scenery by which it is surrounded, make it a most desirable location for the invalid.

Under the superior management of Dr. Gleason, and his accomplished lady, it has become one of the most popular in the Northern States, and its popularity is constantly increasing. Patients have been received from all but five States, and from Upper and Lower Canada.

The names of the Earlier Settlers who have held important positions in the counties of Tioga and Chemung, may be interesting to their descendants. It is difficult to separate the two counties and do justice to all.

The Members of Assembly from Tioga and Chemung, from the organization of each, are as follows:

TIOGA COUNTY.

1792 John Fitch.
1793 John Patterson.
1794 Vincent Mathews.
1795 Vincent Mathews.
1796 Emanuel Coryell.
1797 Emanuel Coryell.
1798 Emanuel Coryell, Benjamin Hovey.
1799 Matthew Carpenter.
1800 Samuel Tinkham.
1801 Edward Edwards.
1802, 1803 Caleb Hyde.
1804 Ashbel Welles.
1805, 1806, 1807 John Miller.
1808, 1809, 1810 Emanuel Coryell.
1811 Thomas Floyd.
1812 Henry Wells.
1813 Jabez Beers.

1814, 1815 Caleb Baker.
1816, 1817, 1818 Gamaliel H. Barstow.
1819 Henry Wells.
1820 Hudson Jennings.
1821 Samuel Lawrence.
1822 Jared Patchen.
1823 Matthew Carpenter, Benjamin Jennings.
1824 Grant B. Baldwin, G. H. Barstow.
1825 Charles Pumpelly, Samuel Winton.
1826 Isaac Baldwin, Anson Camp.
1827 David Williams, G. H. Barstow.
1828 William Maxwell, Jacob Swartwood.
1829 Caleb Baker, Samuel Baragar.
1830 J. G. McDowell, Wright Dunham.
1831 J. G. McDowell, David Williams.
1832 Nathaniel Smith, Joel Tallmadge, Jr.
1833 Jacob Westlake, Thomas Farrington.
1834 John R. Drake, Geo. Gardner.
1835 Geo. Fisher, Green Bennett.
1836 E. H. Goodwin, W. H. Sutton.
[DIVISION IN 1836.]
1837 Ezra Canfield.
1838 John Coryell.
1839 Wright Dunham.
1840 Thos. Farrington
1841 Washington Smith.
1842 John McQuigg.
1843 Simeon R. Griffin.
1844 Nathaniel W. Davis.
1845, 1846 Gideon O. Chase.
1847 Charles R. Barstow.
1848 Erastus Goodrich.
1849 E. S. Sweet.
1850 Isaac Lott.
1851 James Ely.
1852 William Pierson.
1853 T. J. Chatfield.
1855 Lewis P. Legg.
1856 Abram H. Miller.

CHEMUNG COUNTY—MEMBERS OF ASSEMBLY.

1837 Jacob Westlake.
1838 Hiram White.
1839 J. P. Couch.
1840 Guy Hulett.
1841 Jefferson B. Clark.
1842, 1843 S. G. Hathaway, Jr.
1844 S. Hazen.
1845 Peter McKey.
1846 Abm. Primmer.
1847 William Maxwell.
1848 G. W. Buck.
1849 Alva Nash.
1850 Philo Jones.
1851 Samuel Minier.
1852 Jas. B. Van Etten.
1853 H. W. Jackson.
1854 John Randall.
1855 Orrin Robinson.
1856 J. Burr Clark.
1857 Wm. T. Hastings.
1858 John Haggerty.
1859 Lucius Robinson.
1860 Lucius Robinson.
1861 Tracy Beadle.
1862 Charles Hulett.

HISTORY OF ELMIRA.

DISTRICT ATTORNEYS—TIOGA COUNTY.

1818 to June 1822, John L. Tillinghast.
1822 to 1823, William Maxwell.
1823 to 1826, Eleazer Dana.
1826 to 1835, A. Konkle.
1835 to July 1836, A. K. Gregg.

FIRST JUDGES—TIOGA COUNTY.

Abraham Miller 1791 to 1798.
John Patterson 1798 to 1807.
John Miller 1807 to 1810.
Emanuel Coryell 1810 to 1818.
G. H. Barstow 1818 to 1828.
Grant B. Baldwin 1828 to 1833.
John R. Drake 1833 to 1838.

CHEMUNG COUNTY—FIRST JUDGES.

Jos. L. Darling 1836 to 1844.
James Dunn 1844 to 1846.
Jos. L. Darling 1846 to 1847.
J. W. Wisner 1847 to Nov. 1850.
A. Konkle Nov. 1850 Jan. 1851.
A. S. Thurston 1851 to ——.
E. P. Brooks present incumbent.

DISTRICT ATTORNEYS—CHEMUNG COUNTY.

A. K. Gregg 1836 to 1841.
H. Gray 1861, April to July.
D. C. Woodcock 1841 to 1844.
W. North 1844 to 1845.
E. P. Brooks 1845 to 1847.
E. P. Hart 1847 to 1850.
E. Quin 1850 to 1855.
A. Robertson 1855 to 1856.
S. B. Tomlinson, 1856 to 1859.

COUNTY CLERKS—TIOGA COUNTY.

Thos. Nicholson Feb. 1791 to Jan. 13, 1792.
Matthew Carpenter Jan. 1792 to 27th March 1819.
Thos. Maxwell March 1819 to Jan. 1, 1829.
Green M. Tuthill Jan. 1829 to Jan. 1835.
D. Wallis Jan. 1835 to Jan. 1843.
M. Stevens Nov. 1843 to Jan. 1853.
L. W. Kingman Jan. 1, 1853.

COUNTY CLERKS—CHEMUNG COUNTY.

Isaac Baldwin Nov. 1837 to Nov. 1840.
S. L. Rood, Nov. 1840 to Nov. 1846.
G. M. Tuthill Nov. 1846 to Nov. 1849.
A. F. Babcock Nov. 1849 to Nov. 1855.
Richard Baker Nov. 1855 to Nov. 1858.
U. S. Lowe Nov. 1858 to Nov. 1861.
S. B. Tomlinson Jan. 1862

SHERIFFS—TIOGA COUNTY.

Jas. McMasters Feb. 17 1791 to 18th Feb. 1795.
Jos. Hinchman Feb. 18 1795 to 1799.
Edward Edwards 1799 to 1800.
Guy Maxwell Feb. 1800 to Jan. 1804.
John Cantine Jan 1804 to Jan 1805.
Wm. Woodruff Jan. 1805 to Apr. 5 1806.
Wm. Jenkins April 1806 to Feb. 1810.
Jon'a Platt Feb. 1810 to Feb. 1811.
Miles Forman Feb. 1811 to March 1813.
Jon'a Platt March 1813 to April 1815.
Miles Forman April 1815 to March 1819.
E. S. Hinman March 1819 to July 1819.
Henry Wells July 1819 to Feb. 1821.
Miles Forman Feb. 1821 to Nov. 1822.
Wm. Jenkins Nov. 1822 to Nov. 1825.
E. Shoemaker Nov. 1825 to Nov. 1828.
H. McCormick Nov. 1828 to Nov. 1831.
Lyman Covell Nov. 1831 to Nov. 1834.
John Jackson Nov. 1834 to Nov. 1837.

CHEMUNG COUNTY—SHERIFFS.

A. A. Beckwith Nov. 1837 to Nov. 1840.
Samuel Minier Nov. 1840 to Nov. 1843.
William R. Judson Nov. 1843 to Nov. 1846.
William Skellinger Nov. 1846 to Nov. 1849.
William T. Reeder Nov. 1849 to Nov. 1852.
Daniel F. Pickering Nov. 1852 to Nov. 1855.
William M. Gregg Nov. 1858 to Nov. 1861.
William Halliday Nov. 1861.

SENATORS.

The first Senator from the Southern Tier in the Western District was Vincent Mathews, 20th Session 1796 and 1797. 22d Session '98 '99 and 1800. 24th do. 1801 and 1802.
Caleb Hyde 1804, 5, 6, 7 and 8.
Henry A. Townsend 1811 to 1814.
Farrand Stranahan 1815 to 1816.
G. H. Barstow 1819 to 1822.
S. G. Hathaway, F. Stranahan 1823.
L. A. Burrows 1824 to 1827.
G. H. Wheeler 1828 to 1831.
J. G. McDowell 1832 to 1835.
Eben Mack 1836 to 1838.
D. S. Dickinson 1837 to 1840.
A. B. Dickinson 1840 to 1844.
Nehemiah Platt 1841 to 1844.
Wm. M. Hawley 1848.
F. R. Cornell 1852.
G. B. Guinnup 1850.
W. J. Gilbert 1851.
A. B. Dickinson 1854.

CONGRESSMEN.

Of the members of Congress, none appear from this section until the 11th Congress, 1809 to 1811.

Vincent Mathews.
Uri Tracy, 1812 to 1813.
O. C. Comstock, 1813 to 1815.
Daniel Avery, 1813 to 1815.
E. T. Throop, 1815 to 1817.
Daniel Avery, 1815 to 1817.
John R. Drake, 1817 to 1819.
O. C. Comstock, "   "
Caleb Baker, 1819 to 1821.
D. Woodcock, 1821 to 1823.
Samuel Lawrence, 1823 to 1825.
Chas. Humphrey, 1825 to 1827.
D. Woodcock, 1827 to 1829.
Thomas Maxwell, 1829 to 1831.
G. H. Barstow, 1831 to 1833.

S. G. Hathaway, } 1833 to 1835.
N. Halsey,
S. B. Leonard, 1835 to 1837.
A. D. W. Bruyn, 1837 to 1839.
Hiram Gray, 1837 to 1839.
S. B. Leonard, 1839 to 1841.
Samuel Partridge, 1841 to 1843.
Smith M. Purdy, 1843 to 1845.
Stephen Strong, 1845 to 1847.
Wm. T. Lawrence, 1847 to 1849.
S. S. Ellsworth, 1845 to 1847.
Wm. T. Jackson, 1849 to 1851.
H. S. Walbridge, 1851 to 1853.
Andrew Oliver, 1853 to 1855.
Andrew Oliver, 1855 to 1857.

TRINITY CHURCH, Elmira, is located on the corner of Main and Church streets. This edifice was commenced in 1855 and completed in 1858. Seats six hundred persons. A brick building; cost $20,000. The organization was in 1833. The first Rector was Rev. Thomas Clark; present Rector, Rev. Andrew Hull. Communicants, one hundred and sixty. Sunday School one hundred and thirty scholars, twelve female and five male teachers. Francis Collingwood, Superintendent.

Wardens—Harvey Luce, B. P. Beardsley,

Vestry—William P. Yates, Dorus Hatch, John Arnot, Jr., E. H. Benn, V. B. Read, J. R. Lawrence, G. L. Smith, Francis Collingwood.

SAINTS PETER AND PAUL CATHOLIC CHURCH—Located on Corner of Cross and High Streets; number of members, 3,000; edifice built in 1854, 130 by 60, of brick; cost $35,000. First Pastor, Rev. Patrick Brady; present, Rev. M. Kavanaugh.

Sunday School—John Byrne, Superintendent; 10 male teachers, 20 female teachers; male scholars, 175, female scholars, 225.

FIRST PRESBYTERIAN CHURCH—Organized 1793; first Pastor, Rev. Daniel Thatcher; present Pastor, Rev. George C. Curtis, D. D.; **members, 278**; brick building now erecting, corner of Baldwin and

Church streets; entire length, including Lecture Room, 132 **feet**; width of Church edifice, 62 feet; Lecture Room, 35 by 78 feet.

Sunday School, Superintendent, J. Redfield; 10 male, 23 **female teachers**; number of scholars, 60 males, 115 females.

SECOND PRESBYTERIAN CHURCH—Organized 1860; location, corner of Church and Lake streets; edifice built in 1862, of brick, 70 by 90; cost $20,000; first Pastor, Rev. David Murdoch; members, 148.

Sunday School, Superintendent, D. Thompson Dunn : 8 male, 20 female teachers; scholars, 85 male, 118 females.

FIRST METHODIST EPISCOPAL CHURCH—Location on Baldwin street, between Second and Church; Pastor, James E. Latimer; organized, ———; present edifice was built in 1851, of brick, 54 by 76; cost $10,000.

Sunday School, Superintendent, Elias S. Huntley; teachers, 10 male, 13 females; scholars, 60 male, 100 females.

SECOND METHODIST—HEDDING CHURCH—Church street, between College Avenue and Columbia; members present, 200; built in 1852, brick; cost $20,000; first Pastor, Wm. H. Goodwin, D. D; present Pastor, Rev. Edwin J. Hermans.

Sunday School, Superintendent, David Decker; teachers, 8 male, 8 females; scholars, 40 male, 60 females.

AFRICAN METHODIST EPISCOPAL ZION CHURCH—Built in 1852, 30 by 40, wood; cost $1,000; first Pastor, John Tappen; present, James H. Smith.

INDEPENDENT CONGREGATIONAL CHURCH—Organized in 1845; first Pastor, F. W. Graves; present, T. K. Beecher, D. D.; edifice built in 1858, 90 by 65; cost $9,000; members, 240.

Sunday School, Superintendent, Charles T. Farrar; teachers, 8 male 21 females; scholars, 70 male, 90 females.

FIRST BAPTIST CHURCH—Location, Church street, between Wisner and Main; organized in May, 1829; first Pastor, Philander D. Gillett; number of members, 221; edifice built in 1848; wood, stuccoed; cost $8,000; present Pastor, Rev. T. O. Lincoln, D. D.

Sunday School, Superintendent, N. P. Fassett; teachers, 8 male, 21 females; scholars, 82 male, 127 female.

CENTRAL BAPTIST CHURCH—Church street, corner of Church and Conongue; organized in 1859; edifice built in 1860, of brick, 54 by 80; cost $10,000; first Pastor, Rev. J. R. Wilson; present, (supply) S. M. Broakman.

Sunday School, Superintendent, B. P. Fenner; teachers, 5 male, 17 females; scholars, 45 male, 75 females.

YOUNG MEN'S CHRISTIAN ASSOCIATION—Organized in 1858; number of members at organization, 45; present number, 202; Reading Room in Ely's Hall; 30 newspapers, 12 magazines.

OFFICERS.

President—M. S. Converse.
Vice President—W. J. Moulton.
Recording Secretary—T. W. Elmore.
Corresponding Secretary—C. C. Hall.
Treasurer—S. R. Van Campen.

BOARD OF MANAGERS.

M. S. Converse,	W. J. Moulton,
T. W. Elmore,	C. C. Hall,
S. R. Van Campen,	S. Rose, Jr.,
I. F. Hart,	William Dundas,
E. N. Frisbie,	A. S. Clark.

Reading Room open daily, from 8 a. m. to 9 p. m. Free to all. Strangers especially invited to avail themselves of the privileges of the reading room.

THE FIRE DEPARTMENT of Elmira is well and efficiently organized, and reflects much credit on the enterprize and public spirit of the citizens.

BOARD OF TRUSTEES.

President—Washington Marsh.
Secretary—F. Collingwood.
Treasurer—W. P. Yates.

No. 1 Hook & Ladder, Washington Marsh and B. F. Hancock.
No. 1 Engine, F. Collingwood and G. A. Gerow.
No. 2 Engine, J. T. Dudley and Burr L. Hendrick.
No. 3 Engine, Ambrose Wise and B. Coleman.
No. 5 Engine, F. C. Steele and O. A. Drury.

Chief Engineer,
WASHINGTON MARSH.

1st. Assistant,
BURR L. HENDRICK.

2d. Assistant,
O. A. DRURY.

COMPANIES.

Protection Hook & Ladder Company No. 1, is located on Cross street; has 72 members.

    Foreman—John Lovell.
    1st. Assistant—Edward Bartholomew.
    2d. Assistant—Theodore A. Allen.
    Secretary—E. B. Pickering.
    Treasurer—F. A. Stowell.

Torrent Engine Company No. 1, is located on Water street; has 70 members.

    Foreman—G. A. Gerow.
    1st. Assistant—B. Gibbs.
    2d. Assistant—J. Hall.
    Secretary—Calvin White.
    Treasurer—W. P. Yates.

Neptune Engine Company No. 2, is located on Water street; has 58 members.

    Foreman—Miles Trout.
    1st. Assistant—Daniel White.
    2d. Assistant—C. B. Stuart.
    Secretary—C. Beadle.
    Treasurer—Burr L. Hendrick.

Red Rover Engine Company No. 3, is located on Water street; has 80 members.

    Foreman—B. Coleman.
    1st. Assistant—W. C. Russell.
    2d. Assistant—P. Clancy.
    Secretary—Robert Shay.
    Treasurer—James Chapman.

Citizen's Engine Company No. 5, is located on South Lake street; has 65 members.

    Foreman—H. Hitchcock.
    1st. Assistant—F. C. Steele,
    2d. Assistant—Philip Farley.
    Secretary—S. G. Stryker.
    Treasurer—Wm. R. Loomis.

SKETCH OF THE PRESS.

A very important auxiliary in promoting the substantial growth and permanence of our industrial, scientific, moral and religious institutions, is the Country Press; without the assistance of which no enterprise can succeed. Although that Press has done and is doing a great work for society in a sphere where no metropolitan journals can compete with it, it is too often left to languish unsupported, owing to the fact that men do not appreciate its great importance until the very moment when they have " an axe to grind" on the editorial grindstone. It is the local journal that gives character and importance to the town or district wherein it is published. We claim for it in this respect, a precedence over all other influences. Its usefulness might be vastly increased, and the interests of community correspondingly promoted, if its efforts to subserve the common welfare were responded to by a generous confidence and patronage, instead of a distrust, at present much too common, of its faithfulness and reliability, indicated by a parsimonious support, grudgingly bestowed.

For many of the facts in this sketch of Elmira Newspapers we are indebted to the *Gazeteer of the State of New York*, published by R. Pearsall Smith in 1860.

PUBLISHER.

The first paper published in Chemung County, (then Tioga) was at Elmira, (then Newtown) and was called *The Telegraph*, published by Brindle & Murphy, at an early day. (We have not the date of its first issue at hand.) In 1816 its name was changed to *The Vidette*, Brindle & Murphy publishers, subsequently published by William Murphy.

The Investigator was commenced at Elmira in 1820, by Job Smith.— In 1822 its named was changed to *The Tioga Register*, and in 1828 to THE ELMIRA GAZETTE, and its publication continued by Mr. Smith until 1831. It was successively issued by Brinton Paine, Cyrus Pratt, Pratt & Beardsley, Mason & Rhodes, George W. Mason, William C. Rhodes, until 1857, when it passed into the hands of S. C. Taber, by whom it was published until September 1858, when F. A. De Voe purchased the office, and has published the paper unterruptedly since that time.

In August 1856, *The Daily Gazette* was started and continued until June 1857, when it was suspended, and again started in April

1860 by its present proprietor, with Horton Tidd as Editor, who still continues to occupy that position, he having been the Editor of the Weekly Gazette since its purchase by Mr. De Voe.

The Elmira Republican was commenced in 1820 and in 1828 it was changed to *The Elmira Whig*, and published by James Durham. In 1829 it was again changed to *The Elmira Republican*, and published by C. Morgan. It was soon after called *The Elmira Republican and Canal Advertiser*. In 1831 it passed into the hands of John Duffy and its name was changed back to *The Elmira Republican*. It was afterwards issued by Birdsall & Huntley, Ransom & Birdsall, Polleys & Carter, Polleys & Cook, Polleys & Huntley, S. B. & C. G. Fairman, C. G. Fairman, Fairman & Baldwin, Baldwin & Dumars, and Mr. Calhoun, until 1857, when it was discontinued. *The Elmira Daily Republican* was issued a short time in 1846. *The Daily Republican* was issued from the Republican office from the fall of 1851 to 1855.

THE ELMIRA ADVERTISER, Daily and Weekly, was commenced in 1853 by Fairman Brothers. In 1856 F. A. De Voe became pecuniarily interested in it and Fairman & De Voe continued its publication until January 1st, 1863, when Mr. De Voe sold his interest, and S. B. Fairman became the sole proprietor. He continues the publication of the Daily and Weekly with S. B. & C. G. Fairman as Editors.

The Elmira Daily Democrat was issued a short time in 1851 by J. Taylor and S. C. Taber.

The Young American—a journal designed more especially for young people—was published in 1855, by James H. Paine, and was continued nearly a year.

THE DAILY PRESS was established in May, 1859, by Messrs. Dumars, Van Gelder and Paine; subsequently published by Dumars & Van Gelder, R. R. R. Dumars, Dumars & Paine, and was purchased by its present proprietors—Messrs. Thayer & Whitley—in October, 1862.

The Temperance Gem, a monthly publication was issued in Elmira in 1856.

ELMIRA DIRECTORY.

ABBREVIATIONS.

For ab., read *above;* al., *alley;* av., *avenue;* bds., *boards;* bel., *below;* bet., *between;* carp., *carpenter;* cor., *corner;* col'd, *colored;* E., *east;* h., *house;* lab., *laborer;* manuf., *manufacturer;* manufy., *manufactory;* N., *north;* nr., *near;* pl., *place;* propr., *proprietor;* res., *residence;* rd., *road;* S., *south;* W., *west.*

The word *Street* is implied.

A

Abbey G B, barkeeper, h 1 Wyckoff's Block
Abbot Aaron B, railroad conductor, h 3 College av
Abbot Charles R, carriage trimmer, 17 Carroll, h 22 Hudson
Abbott Franklin J, blacksmith, h 51 Water
Abbott William, shoemaker, bds 208 Water
Abraham Lazarus, pedler, h 4 Washington
Adams Jere, h 19 William
Adams John, shoemaker, h Elm nr S Lake
Addison Mrs Abigail, (col'd,) laundress, h 15 Dickinson
Albro Walter H, clerk, bds 38 Gray
Albro Wm W, tobacconist, h 38 Gray
Alexander Minor, tanner, bds 6 S Lake
Allen Asa M, carp, h 24 E Second
Allen John, miller, bds Franklin House
Allen John S, printer, Fairman & DeVoe's Job Printing Office
Allen R R, bridge builder, bds 1 Magee
Allenton John, lab, h 25 Water
Alliston Shadrach, tailor, h 12 DeWitt
Alvord Mrs Hila, h 36 First
Alvord Otis, wool sorter, h 24 Oak
Aman Jacob, brewer, h 104 Baldwin
Ambrose Michael, lab, h 52 College av
American Hotel, Chas I Bush Prop'r, cor Third and Wisner
Anderson F, bridge builder, bds 1 Magee

 **1863.**

SENECA LAKE.

One of the Splendid Low Pressure Steamers,

P. H. FIELD

OR

S. T. ARNOT,

(CAPT. H. TUTHILL,)

Leaves Watkins daily, (Sundays excepted,) on arrival of trains from New York, Philadelphia, Baltimore and Washington, via. Elmira, arriving at Geneva in time for trains east for Albany and New York.

RETURNING,

Leaves Geneva daily, (Sundays excepted,) for Watkins and intermediate places, on arrival of the Train that leaves Albany from the Train and Boats from New York in the morning, connecting with the Night Express at Watkins for Elmira, New York, Philadelphia, Baltimore and Washington.

A. WHEELER,   S. T. ARNOT,
Ag't at Geneva.   Gen. Ag't at Elmira.

☞ The new Steamer Elmira with one of the above Boats will attend to the towing of Canal Boats as usual.

Anderson John G, carp, h 15 Jay
Anderson Wesley, h 5 S Main
Andre John L, tailor, h 70 Church
Andrews H, fireman, bds 1 Magee
Andrews John, saw maker, h 333 Water
Andrews William, saw maker, h 337 Water
Andrus Sylvester G, boarding house, 27 Main
Anhalt Abram, (J A & Co) bds 35 High
Anhalt J & Co, (Julius and Abram Anhalt) wool dealers, 107 Water
Anhalt Julius, (J A & Co) bds 35 High
Ansell William, spinner, h 76 Sullivan
Apt Joseph, propr Hoffman's Hotel, 157 Wisner
ARBOUR HOTEL, Saloon and Billiard Rooms, 7 9 and 11 Lake, Joshua Jones propr
Arburtis Steve, boatman, bds 125 Baldwin
Archer George H, saloon, 172 Water, h same
Armitage Richard F, tinner, 214 Water, h 122 Cross
Armitage William F, dentist, 100 Water, h 214 Church
Armstrong George, (col'd) lab, h Baldwin
Armstrong John, (col'd) lab, h 121 Lake
Armstrong Joseph M, baggage master, h 14 First
Armstrong Mrs Maria M, dress-maker, h 19 E Union
Arnhault Morris, pedlar, h 35 High
Arnold Philip, brewer, h 29 E Union
Arnot John, Pres'dt Chemung Canal Bank, h 57 Lake
Arnot John Jr, Cashier Chemung Canal Bank, h 76 Water
Arnot Mrs Maria, h 17 Hudson
Arnot Matthias H, ass't cashier Chemung Canal Bank, bds 57 Lake
ARNOT STEPHEN T, Vice Pres Chemung Canal Bank, Sup't Elmira GasComp'ny, and propr Seneca Lake Steamers, 5 Lake, h 144 Church
Arnot William H, bds 17 Hudson
Aspinwall Edwin P, book-keeper, bds 49 First
Aspinwall Pomeroy, h 49 First
Assauer Christian, grocer, 27 E Union, h same
Atkins Christopher C, tailor, cor Lake and Water, h 280 Water
Atkins Christopher C Jr, cigar maker, bds 280 Water
Atkins Robert T, cigar maker, bds 280 Water
Atkins William, lab, h S Main nr Franklin
Atkinson Frank H, book-keeper, bds 92 Cross
Atwater Dwight, coal dealer, bds 66 Main
Averill Levi, h cor Church and High
Ayrault Miles, sup't Elmira Water co, office with S R Van Campen, bds Brainard House
Ayres Jehial T, cigar maker, h Hudson bet S Main and Harmon
Ayres Miss Martha, dressmaker, bds 5 Ann
AYRES SOCRATES, watchmaker and jeweler and insurance agent, 99 Water, h 84 Lake

B

Babcock Erastus F, lawyer and Ass't Assessor U S Internal Revenue, 160 Water, bds 32 Main.

COOK & COVELL,

(Successors to Watrous & Cook,)

Hardware Merchants,

MANUFACTURERS OF

Tin, Sheet-Iron & Copper-Ware,

PLUMBERS AND GAS-FITTERS.

Have always on hand a Full stock of

Iron Steel and Nails,
    Paints, Oils and Glass,
        Mechanics' Tools,
            Builders' Hardware,
Wrought Iron Pipe & Fittings, &c., &c.

NOS. 101 & 103 WATER STREET,

FOOT OF LAKE,

ELMIRA, N. Y.

Babcock George, machinist, bds Bevier House
Babcock John G, carp, h 36 Orchard
Bacon William, axe grinder, h 21 S Water
Badger Harwood M, h 48 Factory
Badger L M, watches and jewelry, 103 Wisner, h 31 Fourth
Badger Russell M, lab, h 59 College av
Bailey Columbia, h 72 Gray
Bailey Francis, (col'd) barber, 19 Lake, h same
Bailey Henry L, tanner, bds 56 Factory
Bailey Isaac H, butcher, h 19 Columbia
Bailey James E, wagon-maker, h 4 Conongue
Bailey Timothy, shoemaker, bds 15 S Lake
Baker Miss Ann J, h 55 Water
Baker Francis, lab, h 75 Water
Baker Frederick, brick maker, h 17 Fifth
Baker George, farmer, bds 47 Hudson
Baker Hamilton, bds 47 Hudson
Baker Henry, h 15 High
Baker James M, restaurant, 190 Water, h same
Baker Jonathan G, clerk, bds 12 Hudson
Baker John S, toll-keeper, Lake st Bridge, h 3 S Lake
Baker Leroy, bds 47 Hudson
Baker Nathan, marble dealer, 79 Water, h 40 Water
Baker Richard, h 47 Hudson
Baker Sparrow, butcher, 194 Water, h 28 Hudson
Baldwin Alexander H, ice dealer and lumberman, bds Haight's Hotel
Baldwin Elisha G, printer, h 9 Harmon
Baldwin Gordon W, bds 70 Lake
Baldwin Henry, exp messenger, h 27 Gray
Baldwin J Davis, coal dealer, 112 Cross, h 70 Lake
Baldwin John S, ice dealer, h river rd, Southport
Baldwin Thomas D, (B & Reynolds) h 44 First
Baldwin William I, clerk, bds 70 Lake
BALDWIN & REYNOLDS (Thomas D B, Samuel N R) merchant tailors, 149 Water
Bales William S, carp, h 29 First
Ball Jonathan, Sup't Elmira Umbrella manu'fg co, h 24 W Union
Ballard W W & co, (William W B, Joseph C Sampson) oil barrel manufy 164 Church
Ballard William W, (W W B & co) h 42 Baldwin
Baltz John F, cooper, h 4 Gray
Baltz Richard D, cooper, h 76 Baldwin
Bank of Chemung, Tracy Beadle Pres'dt, Ralph W Beadle cashier, Henry W Beadle ass't cashier, 130 Water
Barber Abbott, mason, h 93 First
Barber James W, mason, h 17 Sullivan
Barbour Elijah N, butter dealer, h 255 Church
Barentlar P, saloon, 84 Wisner cor Second, h same
Barker James M, shoemaker, bds 93 Cross
Barnes David, carp, h 345 Water
Barnes William H, (Thomas & B) bds National Hotel

ELMIRA STEAM MILLS.

WM. HALLIDAY, & Co.,

Wholesale and Retail Dealers in

Flour, Grain, Meal, Mill Feed, &c.

Custom Work Done on Short Notice.

ELMIRA, N. Y.

WM. HALLIDAY. E. C. MERRILL.

Barnes Willis S, oyster dealer, bds Brainard House
Barnett Jeremiah, lab, h Fulton bet Hudson and River
Barnett John, lab, h 30 Hatch
Barney Henry, bds 9 S Water
Barney Joseph H, clerk, h 9 S Water
Barr Gabriel, intelligence office, 56 Lake, h same
Barr Nicholas, lab, h 1 Canal
Barrett Warren S, h Tuthill av, nr Factory
Barry David, lab, h Walnut, nr Hudson
Barry John, lab, h 14 Henry
Barth Ferdinand, carp, h 19 First
Bartholomew Edmund, carp, bds 49 Baldwin
Bartholomew Josiah, carp, h 48 Baldwin
Bartholomew Oscar N, carp, h 20 Orchard
BARTHOLOMEW URIAH, tobacconist, 9 Baldwin, boards Brainard House
Bartholph Andrew, blacksmith, h 67 Gray
Barton R Walter, (B & Dickinson) h cor Baldwin and Third
Barton & Dickinson, (R Walter B, George S D) grocers, 8 Lake
Bateman Mrs Eliza, h 56 Washington
Bates James, mason, h Partridge, nr S Main
Bauer Charles, iron worker, h 119 Lake
Bauer George, bds 119 Lake
Beach William, h 24 William
Beadle Chauncey M, clerk, bds 86 Lake
Beadle Henry W, ass't Cashier Bank of Chemung, bds 88 Lake
Beadle Ralph W, Cashier Bank of Chemung, bds 86 Lake
Beadle Tracy, Pres't Bank of Chemung, h 86 Lake
Beaman M, bridge builder, bds 1 Magee
Bean George, tanner, h 3 N Oak
Bean Martin, clerk, bds 19 Wisner
Beardsley Benoni P, edge tool manuf, 50 Lake, h 92 Cross
Beardsley Elisha J, teacher, h S Water bet Harmon and Main
Bechtol Hiram, shoemaker, h 44 Clinton
Beck Mrs Rosanna, h cor Fourth and Dickinson
Beckwith George, farmer, h 230 Hoffman
Beckwith James B, dyer, 51 Water, h same
Bedell Horace, (Cook, Willis, B & Co) h 59 Baldwin
Bedine Daniel S, wagon maker, bds 6 Washington
Beebe George, lawyer, 4 Lake, h 4½ Ann
Beecher Rev Thomas K, Pastor Congregational Church, h Factory nr Water Cure
Beers E O, Capt N Y Vol, bds 323 Water
Beers George, carp, h 318 Water
Beers Johnson, (Elmendorf & B) h cor John and DeWitt
Beers William, carp, h 323 Water
Bell Andrew W, iron worker, h cor Willow and Washington av
Bell M Addison, carp, h 166 Water
Belton Samuel, blacksmith, h 62 High
Bement Rev William, h 76 Washington av
Benedict James, carp, h cor Broadway and Main
Benjamin Henry L, physician, h 38 Main

T. S. PATTINSON,
BUTCHER & OYSTER PACKER

Wholesale & Retail Dealer in

Oysters---Cans, Gallons, Counts,

FRESH FISH, GAME, &c., any quantity.

Orders attended to at the shortest notice.

MARKET, No. 123 Water Street, Elmira, N. Y.

W. J. LORMORE,

No. 25 Lake-St., Elmira, N. Y.

DEALER IN

GROCERIES & PROVISIONS,

PORK, FISH, FLOUR, FEED, OATS,

WOOD & WILLOW-WARE,

Foreign & Domestic Fruits,

Cigars, Tobacco, &c., &c.

☞ Goods delivered to all parts of the Village—Free of Charge.

Benjamin James H, clerk, bds 108 Lake
Benjamin Simeon, Vice Pres'dt Elmira Rolling Mill Co, 130 Water, h 96 Lake
Benjamin William F, clerk and steward Female College, h 108 Lake
Benn Erastus H, lawyer, 20 Lake, h 30 First
Bennett Albert P, h 31 De Witt
Bennett Miss Frances L, (Cole & B) bds 50 Cross
Bennett Mrs Rheuby, h 292 Water
Bennett Solomon, lumber manuf, h 37 Main
Bennett Wm H, law student, bds 60 Sullivan
Benson Joseph, lab, bds 27 Water
Benson William, lab, bds 27 Water
Benton Henry P, surveyor, h 13 Gray
Berhalter Joseph, shoemaker, 105 Church, h same
Bermingham Mrs Mary, h 11 E Third
Bermingham Michael, lab, h 9 E Third
Berner Adam, vinegar manuf, 30 Water, h same
Berry David, carp, h 14 Sullivan
Bertholf Theodore, clerk, bds Gray cor Davis
Bessy John, carp, h 281 Church
Betson Peter, lab, h 12 N Oak
Bettridge Henry E, baker, h 82 Church
Bevier Edgar, porter, Delavan House
Bevier Henry H, (B & Briggs) h 260 Water
Bevier House, O C Walters Prop'r, 117 Wisner
Bevier & Briggs, (Henry H Bevier, Thomas Briggs) brewers and malsters Second nr Wisner
Bidwell Gilbert, (B & Moshier) h cor S Lake and Mt Zoar
Bidwell & Moshier, (Gilbert B, Humphrey J M) meat market cor Church and Wisner
Bigelow William A, (B & Richardson) h 11 S Lake
Bigelow & Richardson, (William A B, Jackson R) boots and shoes, Water nr Wisner
Biggs Miss Mary, milliner, Holden's Hall, bds 79 Baldwin
Biggs Peter, (Kelly, B & Co) h 79 Baldwin
Billett Francis, lab, bds 76 Gray
Billett Joseph, grocer, 188 Water, h 222 Church
Billett Theodore, moulder, h 76 Gray
Billings David T, produce dealer, h 78 Gray
Billings John L, grocer, 32 Water, h same
Bingham Almerin, hatter, Stuart & Ufford, h S Water
Bingham John, carp, bds 37 S Water
Bird Isaac, (col'd) lab, h 30 S Lake
Birdsall Oliver, grocer, 47 Main, h 54 Main
Birmingham James, lab, h 78 Baldwin
Birmingham John, lab, h 48 College av
Bishop Mrs Mary, h 44 Clinton
Bishop Vincent, lab, h 12 N Oak
Bissell William D, blacksmith, with C L Davis
Blaisdell Stephen, cancer doctor, bds 208 Water
Blake Abijah, h 44 S Water
Blake Elial B, umbrella cutter, h 27 College av

E. LEHMAN & CO.,

MERCHANT TAILORS

AND DEALERS IN

CLOTHING,

FURNISHING GOODS,

Cloths, Cassimeres, Vestings, &c.

No. 151 WATER STREET,

Elmira, N. Y.

Opposite Brainard House.

Particular Attention given to Custom Tailoring.

Blake Jonathan, bds cor Lake and Washington av
Blake John, lab, h 209 Wisner
Blampied John, hackman, h 219 Church
Blampied Joshua, baker and grocer, 196 Water, h 107 Wisner
Bliven Asa, (B & Jewett) h 39 Wisner
Bliven George, machinist, at 181 Church
Bliven & Jewett, (Asa B, Thomas M J Jr) iron manuf, cor Wisner and Church
Blodgett Gardner A, lab, h 50 Gray
Bloss Francis, boots & shoes, 27 Union, bds Western Hotel
Bloss Martin, shoemaker, h 27 Jay
Blossom Enos, bds Brainard House
Bly Norman, teller Bank of Chemung, bds Brainard House
Boake James, lab, h 92 Second
Boardley Mrs Catherine, (col'd) bds 14 Perry
Bochnievetch Joseph, saloon, 73 Water, h same
Bodine John S, wagon maker, bds Washington
Bogart James, bds Haight's Hotel
Bogart Louis, N Y Vol, h 8 Hatch
Bohan James, shoemaker, bds S Water
Bolt Martin S, grocer, 50 Second, h same
Bolton S, h Second nr Wisner
Bookmyer Frederick, book-binder, 117 Water, h 42 High
Boothe Elijah, carp, h 2 Ann
Bopp Jacob, butcher, h 8 Henry
Borden A F, machinist, bds American Hotel
Bortle Ephraim, restaurant, 192 Water, h same
Bottsford Shelden, mason, bds 27 Conongue
Bovier James M, clerk, h S Lake
Bow William, carp, bds 67 Fifth
Bowman George R, shoemaker, bds 206 Water
Bowman Henry, tanner, h 289 Water
Bowman James W, sawyer, h 1 Mt Zoar
Bower George, (B & Romer) bds National Hotel
Bower & Romer, (George B, Anthony R) merchant tailors, 119 Water
Boynton Austin H, lumberman, bds Haight's Hotel
Braack Peter, piano maker, bds cor Wisner and Cross
Bradman Charles, h Washington av
Bradshaw Aaron, h Sly's Plot
Bradshaw Alfred, lab, bds Sly's Plot
Bradshaw George, engineer, at 12 Wisner
Bradshaw Henry, lab, h S Lake nr Miller
Bradshaw Henry H, cigar-maker, bds Sly's Plot
Brady Peter, cooper, h 23 S Water
Branch Edwin, blacksmith, h 12 Hudson
Brand John, (B & Hoffman) and grocer and butcher, 1 S Lake, h same
Brand & Hoffman, (John B, Henry H) distillers, Buttonwoods
Brant Sandy, (col'd) lab, h 34 Clinton
Breen Patrick, iron-worker, bds 36 Hatch
Brees Elias, ostler, bds 32 Baldwin
Brenan Patrick, lab, h Davis bet Fifth and Sixth
Brewer Lucas, cabinet-maker, h 40 Wisner

TUTHILL, BROOKS & CO,

DEALERS IN

DRY GOODS,

132 WATER STREET,

ELMIRA, N. Y.

D. H. TUTHILL.   H. S. BROOKS.   E. B. SATTERLEE.

ALSO,

CHOICE FAMILY GROCERIES.

Brickwedde Ferdinand, tinner, bds 24 Washington
Brickwedde George, clerk, bds 24 Washington
Brickwedde Henry tinner, h 24 Washington
Bridgeman Lewis H, millwright, h 347 Water
Briesley George, painter, bds 60 College av
Briggs Benjamin H, h 56 Washington
Briggs I P, blacksmith, h 264 Water
Briggs Smith, carp, h 1 S Magee
Briggs Smith F, machinist, bds 1 S Magee
Briggs Thomas, (Bevier & B) h 97 Lake
Brink D H, h 206 Church
Brink George W, agt newsroom, 120 Water, bds 206 Church
Brink Miss Mary A, newsroom, 120 Water, res Aurora N Y
Britton Mrs Emma, h 8 Perry
Britton J D, salt dealer, bds American Hotel
Broakman Judson J, clerk, bds 38 Cross
Broakman Samuel M, pastor Central Baptist Church, h 38 Cross
Brockmuller John C, florist, cor William and E Third, h same
Brockway Daniel S, clerk, bds 199 Water
Brockway Joseph T, fish market, 199 Water, h same
Broder John, tailor, h 48 Wisner
Brodman Charles, iron-worker, Rolling Mill
Brody Thomas, lab, h 69 High
Bronson Henry, carp, h 88 First
Brook James C, woolen manuf, h 22 College av
Brookman J Judson, clerk, bds 22 Washington
Brooks Caleb B, lab, h 12 Henry
Brooks Elijah P, lawyer and Co judge, Court House, h 91 Coll'ge av
Brooks Henry S, (Tuthill, B & Co) h 20 William
Brooks Warren, iron-worker, bds 2 Hatch
Brooks Warren W, iron worker, h 133 Lake
Brown Caleb, (col'd) lab, h 109 Baldwin
Brown Miss Caroline, (col'd) laundress, h 8 Perry
Brown Comfort S, teacher, h 10 Harmon
Brown Daniel B, lab, h 2 E Third
Brown David B, carrier Gazette, h 294 Water
Brown David H, mason, bds 27 Conongue
Brown DeWitt C, cigar maker, h 37 Water
Brown George S, stone cutter, bds 34½ Baldwin
Brown Guy P, butcher, h 3 Ann
Brown Horace, mason, h 4 Orchard
Brown Jefferson, (col'd) whitewasher, h 2 E Second
Brown John, (col'd) lab, h Franklin nr Fulton
Brown John, hatter, h 3 Ann
Brown John S, (col'd) lab, bds 106 Baldwin
Brown Mrs Maria S, h 34½ Baldwin
Brown Mrs Mary E, (col'd) cook, h 1 Fourth
Brown Mrs Rachel, (col'd) laundress, h 110 Baldwin
Brown Samuel, boatman, h 4 Columbia
Brown Solomon, (col'd) waiter, Brainard House
BROWN WM, hardware 14 and 16 Lake, bds Brainard House
Brown Wm, (col'd) lab, h Dickinson

S. B. HUBBELL,

Manufacturer of, and Wholesale and Retail Dealer in

Furniture & Upholstery

OF ALL DESCRIPTIONS.

LOOKING GLASSES, PICTURE FRAMES,

FEATHERS, SPRING BEDS, &C.

WARE ROOMS No 174 WATER-ST., Union Block,

[NEXT TO THE CANAL.]

ELMIRA, N. Y.

UNDERTAKING

In all its branches attended to promptly.

Brown Zalmon, painter, bds 31 Conongue
Browne Jacob W, clerk Erie Railway, h 23 First
Browne Wm H, machinist, h 24 College av
Bruen John H, h 51 Fourth
Brush George A, lawyer, 157 Water, h cor Church and Columbia
Bryant Lewis W, agent, h 51 Washington
Buckley Patrick, shoemaker, h Hudson bet Harmon and Fulton
Bulmer David, dry goods and groceries, 108 Water, boards Brainard House
Bulloch John, bookkeeper, h 202 Church
Bundy George, (col'd) lab, h 15 Dickinson
Bundy Jaben A, (O F & J A B) h 38 Washington
Bundy O F & J A, (Oscar F, Jaben A) grocers, 37 Lake
Bundy Oscar F, (O F & J A B) h 38 Washington
Burbage John, shoemaker, 191 Water, h Southport
Burbage Joseph, saw manuf, h 53 Gray
Burch Erastus, cabinet maker, h 32 Fourth
Burchell Mrs Catherine, h John nr Harriett
Burchell John, porter Delavan House
Burchell Richard, lab, h 66 Washington
Burchill T, iron worker, Rolling Mill
Burchfield Mrs Nellie, dress maker 170 Water, h same
Burdick Oramel R, local editor *Press*, bds Franklin House
Burk John, lab, h 62 Washington
Burns Dennis, lab, h   Hatch
Burns Martin, lab, h   Wisner
Burns Patrick, lab, h 48 Magee
BURNS THOMAS, grocer 95 Water, h 34 S Water
Burt Albert, cooper, bds Wisner
Burt Garry A, billiard marker, bds Elmira Hotel
Burton Mrs Seville, cloak maker, 28 Lake, h same
Bush ——, (Shiedlen & B) h Water nr Gas Works
Bush C N, engineer, bds 1 Magee
Bush Charles, carp, h 3 Dickinson
Bush Charles I, propr American Hotel cor Third and Wisner
Bush William, pedler, h 22 Water
Butcher Edward, shoemaker, h 3 Gregg
Butler John, lab, h 79 Fifth
Butler Thomas, lab, h 20 Water
Butler Martin, hackman, h 95 Fifth
Butler Mrs Mary, h 48 Sullivan
Butler Nicholas, machinist at 181 Church
Butler William F, teamster, bds 48 Sullivan
Butterlee Mrs Jane, h 102 Main
Byrne John, cooper, h 20 First

C

Cahill Edward, lab, h 34 E Second
Cahill John, barkeeper, bds 49 Cross
Cahill John, saloon, h 82 Wisner
Cahill Michael, lab, h 49 Cross

S. S. HUTCHINSON,

(Successor to N. H. Robinson,)

CASH DEALER IN

BOOTS & SHOES,

No. 126 Water Street, Elmira, N. Y.

Gentlemens' French Calf Boots

of the very best style and quality, made promptly to order.

N. W. GARDINER,

Manufacturer of and Dealer in

HATS, CAPS & FURS,

GLOVES & MITTENS,

—ALSO—

BUFFALO ROBES,

No. 117 Water-St., Elmira, N. Y.

Cash paid for all kinds of Furs.   Silk Hats made to order.

Cahill Thomas, lab, h Wisner bet Fifth and Sixth
Cain Dennis, blacksmith, bds Church
Call Purinton, carriage trimmer, h 13 High
Callagan Patrick, lab, h 73 Main
Callahan Daniel, lab, h foot of Franklin
Caller Burnam, tailor, bds 65 Cross
Cammel Barney, lab, h 5 Hatch
Cammel John, lab, h 12 Canal
Cammel Michael, lab, h Hatch nr Fifth
Camp Marvin, baggage man, bds American Hotel
Campbell Miss E M, teacher, bds 63 Baldwin
Campbell John H, shoemaker, h 37 John
Campbell Joseph A, machinist, bds 107 Lake
Campbell Mrs Mary T, h 107 Lake
Campbell Michael, railroad car inspector, h 36 S Water
Campbell Michael, iron worker, Rolling Mill
Campher James C, (col'd) lab, h 115 Baldwin
Campin Michael, lab, h 32 S Lake
Canby George, bricklayer, h 81 Fifth
Canfield Ezra, lumberman, h 195 Church
Canfield L D, tinner, h S Water
Canoll Charles, railroad ticket agent, h 26 Fourth
Carbarry Edward, lab, at Third Ward Hotel
Carey De Forest B, artist, bds 32 Sullivan
Carey Erastus T, lab, h cor Oak and Fifth
Carey Francis W, tailor, h 32 Sullivan
Carey Michael, gardner, h 63 Gray
Carl Edward A, h 208 Water
Carney Patrick, shoemaker, at 61 Wisner
Carpenter Mrs Calvin, h 272 Church
Carpenter Mrs Charlotte, h 6 N Oak
Carpenter George E, (C, Perry & Co) h 32 William
Carpenter Grant B, harness maker, h 139 Water
Carpenter Nelson, (Williams & C) h 62 Gray
Carpenter, Perry & Co, (George E C, Thomas P, John R Goodrich) glue manufs, Tuthill's av nr Church
Carpenter Robert T, grocer, 100 Water, h 14 S Lake
Carpenter Zenas R, bedstead maker, h 8 Columbia
Carr Barney, lab, h 16 Hatch
Carr Mrs Betsy, h 71 Baldwin
Carr James, lab, h 19 Canal
Car Owen, iron worker, h 3 Seventh
Carr Peter, lab, h 16 Hatch
Carr Silas T, carriage maker, h 11 E Union
Carr William S, clerk, bds 71 Baldwin
Carrier James, shoemaker, h 108 Gray
Carrier Joseph, carp, h 106 Lake
Carrigan James, lab, h 6 Canal
Carris John, machinist, h 60 College av
Carroll Joseph, cutter merchant tailoring department Stuart & Ufford, h 20 Conongue
Carruthers George, h 43 First

ARBOUR HOTEL.

SALOON,

Restaurant & Billiard Rooms,

JOSHUA JONES, PROPRIETOR.

Nos. 7, 9 & 11, Lake Street.

Separate Rooms for Ladies Up-Stairs---Entrance No. 9.

FIRST CLASS BILLIARD TABLES
and the best of Liquors.

G. W. SCARDEFIELD & CO.,

PRACTICAL GILDERS,

Manufacturers of Plain and Ornamental

LOOKING - GLASS AND PICTURE FRAMES,

AND ALL KINDS OF OVALS,

AND DEALERS IN

LOOKING - GLASS PLATES, &C.,

Opposite the Post Office,

No. 11 BALDWIN-St., - - **ELMIRA, N. Y.**

Old Frames of all kinds Re-Gilt equal to New.

Carter Alva S, painter, h 8 College av
Carter Charles, clerk, h 44 Gray
Carter Levi, (col'd) lab, h 8 Hatch
Cash George P, h 10 W Third
Cashman David T, carriage painter, bds 208 Water
Cass John, merchant tailor, cor Baldwin and Water, h 27 William
Casterlin Horace, gunsmith. bds 18 Conongue
Catchpole William, lab, h 33 Wisner
Cattanger Lewis. tailor, h 33 High
Cauldwell Nathaniel, Commercial College, 159 Water, bds Brainard House
Caywood William, pedler, bds 208 Water
Central Baptist Church, cor Church and Conongue
Ceroll Joseph, tailor, h 20 Conongue
Chamberlin John W, (Vinton & C) h 28 Gray
Chapin Freeman, edge tool maker, h 68 Sullivan
Chapin Mrs Lucy A, h 76 Cross
Chapman James J, machinist, h 18 Henry
Chapman Joshua. bds 2 Fox
Chapman Miss Marcia L, dressmaker, h 2 Fox
Chase Zalmon F, physician, h 2 Conongue
Chemung Canal Bank, John Arnot pres't, Stephen T Arnot vice pres't, John Arnot Jr cash'r, Matthias H Arnot ass't cash'r, 74 Water
Chemung House, Mrs Electa Cherry proprietress, 29 Baldwin
Cherry Mrs Electa, proprietress Chemung House, 29 Baldwin
Cherry Larry, h Partridge nr railroad
Cherry Leonard K, carman, h 11 Dickinson
Cherry Patrick, artist, bds Partridge nr railroad
Chubb Stephen, blacksmith, bds 223 Church
Chubbuck Hollis S, physician 36 Baldwin, h same
Churchill Jackson V, wagon maker, h 6 Henry
Churchill Thomas W, pistol maker, h 204 Church
Churchill Wm, lab, h Franklin nr Fulton
Churchwell Nelson, hackman, bds Brainard House
Clancy Patrick, lab. h First
Clancey James, cigar maker, bds Elmira Hotel
Clark Allen S, clerk, bds 41 First
Clark A B, Williamsport RR agent, bds Delavan House
Clark Mrs Catherine, h 20 De Witt
Clark Damon W, shoemaker, bds 20 De Witt
Clark Ephraim A, lab, h Fulton bet Mt Zoar and Franklin
Clark Ira J, teamster, h 18 Fifth
Clark Rev Isaac, pastor Second Presbyterian church, h 138 Church
Clark J B, lumber manuf. h 203 Church
Clark James F, carp, h Hudson nr Western limits
Clark John, lab, h John bet Washington and Orchard
Clark John C, h 329 Water
Clark Joseph, lab, bds 34 W Union
Clark Julien, Agent Elmira & Williamsport Railroad, bds Delavan House
Clark Sylvenus, carp, h 186 Church

E. WILLIAMS,

DEALER IN ALL KINDS OF

Groceries & Provisions,

FLOUR & FEED,

WILLOW AND WOODEN WARE AND FRUITS,

No. 19 Lake Street, Elmira, N. Y.

ALL KINDS OF PRODUCE BOUGHT AND SOLD.

Clark William, engineer, h 6 Perry
Clark William, butcher, h 23 E Union
Clark Wm B, carp, h 1 Magee
Clark William B, saloon, Delavan House
Cleeves Mrs E J, boarding house, 254 Water
Cleeves Wm B, clerk, bds 254 Water
Clendenny Theodore, moulder, bds 76 Gray
Cleveland Alanson J, lawyer, h 26 S Lake
Cleveland Frank C, baggage man, h 15 Magee
Cleveland James H, foreman Elmira Car Shop, h 47 Cross
Cleveland William H, teacher, bds 72 William
Clifford Alfred, piano maker, h cor Church and High
Close Reuben H, nursery, h cor S Main and Partridge
Clymer Thos, bds Brainard House
Cobett Murty, iron worker, Rolling Mill
Coburn Daniel, baker, h 46 Cross
Coddington Mrs E A, dressmaker, 113 Water, h same
Coe Francis U, shoemaker, bds 115 Church
Coe Henry, fireman, bds Troy House
Coe Isaac H, fireman, bds 115 Church
Coe John D, shoemaker, h 115 Church
Coe William D, shoemaker, bds 115 Church
Cohn Norman, pedler, bds 10 High
COKE LEVI, baker, confectioner and grocer, 31 Lake h same
Coke Philip, baker, h cor Fox and Carroll
Colburn Wells L, agent, h 86 Gray
Cole Mrs Caroline M, (C & Bennett) h 50 Cross
Cole Charles B, agent Empire Brewery, bds American Hotel
Cole Myron, (Huntley & C) h 50 Cross
Cole & Bennett, (Mrs Caroline M C, Miss Frances B) milliners, 114 Water
Coleman A K, carp, h 349 Water
Coleman Benjamin, mason, h 31 DeWitt
Coleman Charles, lab, bds 10 Columbia
Coleman John, carp, h 10 Columbia
Coleman Joseph S, harness maker, h 12 Orchard
Colgrove Miss Sarah, h 85 Water
Coligan Michael, lab, h First
Collingwood Brothers, (Robert and Francis) watchmakers and jewellers, 13 Lake
Collingwood Francis, (C Bros) h 24 First
Collingwood Robert, (C Bros) h 77 John
Collingwood Thomas, clerk, bds 290 Water
Collins John, lab, h 25 Magee
Collins Stephen, iron worker, Rolling Mill
Collins Thomas, cooper, bds Wisner
Comfort Eli C, botanic physician, cor Lake and Carroll
COMSTOCK SAMUEL G, hats, caps, furs, &c, 150 Water,(2 Brainard Block) bds 5 S Main
Condol William H, (col'd) whitewasher, h S Lake nr Miller
Condon John, lab, bds 60 Factory
Condon Mrs Sarah, h 60 Factory
Congdon Erastus, clerk, h 70 Sullivan

RICE, DURLAND & PRATT,

(*Successors to* HAMLIN & RICE,)

DEALERS IN

DRY GOODS,

Carpeting, Rugs, Matting,

OIL CLOTHS,

No. 122 Water Street, Elmira, N. Y.

N. B.····Carpets Cut and Made to Order.

Congdon George, maltster, h 279 Church
Conkey Samuel, (C & French) h 27 W Union
Conkey & French, (Samuel C, Edson M F) dentists, 116 Water
Conkle George H, h 102 Church
Conklin Walter W, engineer, h 13 Hudson
Conklin William W, iron worker, Rolling Mill
Conley Timothy, lab, h nr Hudson
Connell Patrick, lab, h DeWitt nr E Second
Connolly Cornelius, lab, h Walnut nr Hudson
Connolly Daniel, lab, h Hudson bet Fulton and Walnut
Connolly Dennis, lab, h Walnut nr Hudson
Connolly Hugh, Rolling Mill House, 29 Canal
Connolly Jerry, cigar maker, at J I Nicks'
Connolly John, lab, h S Water bet Fulton and Harmon
Connolly John, tailor, h 56 High
Connolly John, lab, h cor Fulton and Hudson
Connolly Michael, lab, h cor Hudson and Mt Zoar
Connolly Patrick, lab, h Walnut nr Hudson
Connolly Patrick, boarding house, 48 Clinton
Connolly Thomas, lab, h Buttonwoods
Connolly Timothy, iron worker, Rolling Mill
Connolly Timothy, cooper, bds Wisner
Converse Maxey M, music teacher, h 75 Lake
Converse Moses S, Principal Young Men's Seminary, 17 William
Cook ——, bridge builder, bds 1 Magee
Cook Elisha H, (C & Covell) h 19 S Water
Cook George J, produce dealer, h 317 Water
Cook Jeremiah, pedler, bds 59 First
Cook John J, printer, bds Elmira Hotel
Cook Sidney S, machinist, h 21 Columbia
Cook Thomas, livery stable Bevier House, bds Bevier House
Cook, Willis, Bedell & Co, (George C, Christopher W, H and D E Bedell, Nelson Chandler, Peter Rhoades) Elmira Oil Refinery, head of Willow
COOK & COVELL, (Elisha H Cook, Henry C Covell) hardware, stoves, &c, 101 and 103 Water
Cooke Frederick J, harness maker, h 33 Sullivan
Cooley Jesse L, bookkeeper S T Arnot, h Horseheads rd ab Canal
Cooley Levi J, police justice, Town Hall, h cor Washington av and Lake
Cooney Daniel, lab, bds 48 College av
Copley Philip, basket maker, h 116 Baldwin
Coppins Reuben, harness maker, bds Chemung House
Corbin Mrs Charlotte, h 7 Orchard
Corbit Wm, (col'd) lab, h Lane nr S Main
Corcoran Thomas, saloon, 25 Canal h same
Cord Primus, (col'd) lab, h 26 Dickinson
Corey Augustus F, corporation collector, 6 Ely Hall, h Elm between S Main and Lake
Corey William F, cashier Elmira Bank, h 209 Church
Cornelison James, printer, bds Haight's Hotel
Cornell Joseph, shoe maker, h 6 Columbia
Cortright Marcus P, cooper, h 12 Hudson

S. G. COMSTOCK,

DEALER IN

Hats, Caps & Furs,

No. 150 Water Street---No. 2 Brainard Block,

ELMIRA, N. Y.

FUR & WOOL HATS, CLOTH & FUR CAPS,

BUFFALO ROBES.

Ladies' Furs, Gloves and Robes,

IN GREAT VARIETY.

STRAW GOODS.

BUCK AND KID GLOVES AND MITTENS,

UMBRELLAS, &C., &C.

Cortright Stephen, iron worker, h 23 Canal
Corwin Louisa F, h 34 College av
Cotrell Stephen H, carp, h 61 College av
Cotton George H, carp, h First av nr S Water
Couch Ebenezer, hatter, bds with Henry S Snyder
Couch Stephen B, grocer, Canal Junction, h same
Coulton Edward V, draughtsman and engineer, h 36 Water
Coulton Edward V Jr, shoemaker, h 36 Water
Courry Mrs Eliza, h Sly's Plot
Courtright ——, lab, h Buttonwoods
Courtright John, cooper, bds 55 William
Covell Edward, (E C & Co) bds Haight's Hotel
COVELL E & CO, (Edward C, Robert C Jr) dry goods and groceries, 106 Water
Covell Henry C, (Cook & C) h 66 Water
Covell Jacob M, bookkeeper, bds 66 Water
Covell James, clerk, bds 72 Lake
COVELL JOHN D, druggist, 102 Water, bds Brainard House
Covell Lyman, h 64 Water
Covell Robert, h 111 College av
Covell Robert Jr, (E C & Co) h 55 Lake
Covell Stephen T, telegraph operator, bds 64 Water
Covell William D, bds 64 Water
Cowen Mrs Mary, h 53 Dickinson
Cowen Newton F, clerk, bds 31 High
Cowen Thaddeus A, (C & Son) bds 31 High
Cowen Thaddeus C, (C & Son) h 31 High
COWEN & SON, (Thaddeus C C, and Thaddeus A C) auction and commission merchants, 12 Lake

Cowles Rev A W, pres't Female College, h 95 College av
Cowles Henry D, clerk, h 4 Main
Cowles Samuel G, with S R Van Campen, bds Brainard House
Cox George H, express messenger, bds Brainard House
Craig M D, bds American Hotel
Craig Peter, carder, bds 62 Factory
Craig Robert B, carder, h 62 Factory
Cramp Robert, lab, h 42 Cross
Crane Abijah, mason, h 63 First
Crane Delivan, painter, h 14 Hudson
Crane Ezra C, boatman, bds 6 E Second
Crane Rev Ezra F, chaplain 107 N Y vols, h 6 E Second
Crane Mrs Hiram, boarding house, 64 Main
Crane Theodore, clerk, bds 27 Main
Craven John, tinner, h 6 DeWitt
Creed James A, h 26 Cross
Creelman Matthew, tailor, h 40 Orchard
Crittenden Richard G, blacksmith, h cor John and High
Cromer Josiah, lab, bds 101 College av
Cronan James, lab, h 65 High
Cronan John, lab, h 67 Washington av
Crosby Walter, clerk, h 75 Baldwin
Cross Edward, cabinet-maker, bds 135 Lake

UNION MILLS.

GARRY H. POST,

Wholesale & Retail Dealer in

Coffees, Teas and Spices,

ARMISTEAD'S AND COLEMAN'S

LONDON MUSTARD,

PURE CREAM TARTAR, SALERATUS, &c.

No. 155 Water Street,

ELMIRA, N. Y.

Cross George, (col'd) lab, bds 95 Cross
Cross Samuel, iron worker, h 135 Lake
Crow Martin, lab, h 20 First
Crowly Michael, lab, h 18 First
Cruger Aaron, (col'd) lab, h 106 Baldwin
Cruger George, (col'd) lab, h 106 Baldwin
Cruttenden Miss Harriett, teacher, h 62 Cross
Cuddeback John, carp, h 349 Water
Cullinan John, iron worker, Rolling Mill
Culp Jacob H, cooper, bds 4 Fox
Culp James B, saloon, 44 Lake, h same
Culp Mrs Harriet, h 4 Fox
Cummin William, carp, h Partridge nr E RR
Cummings Edward, saloon, 59 Wisner, h same
Cummings James, mason, h 16 First
Cummings Marsh, carp. h 13 Jay
Cunan James, iron worker, Rolling Mill
Cunningham Michael, lab, bds 65 Cross
Curly John, lab, h Harriett nr Cross
Curran David, lab, h 10 E Third
Curran James, iron worker, h 12 Hatch
Curran Mrs Sarah A, dressmaker, h 75 Baldwin
Curran Thomas, lab, h 67 High
Curry Michael, lab, h 209 Wisner
Curtin Andrew J, cigar maker, bds cor High and Jay
Curtin Patrick, cigar maker, h cor High and Jay
Curtis Rev George C, pastor First Pres Church, h 40 William

D

Dale William, brakeman, bds 1 Magee
Dalton Michael, iron worker, h 61 Second
Daly Mrs Catharine, h 46 Hudson
Daly Dennis, machinist, h 18 Washington
Daly Patrick, lab, h 7 E Third
Daly Patrick, bds 46 Hudson
Daniels Evern, caulker, h 238 Church
Daniels William H, carp, h 16 Sullivan
Davenport A Barton, tinner, bds 53 Baldwin
Davenport Ephraim, (Gridley & D) h 53 Baldwin
Davidge John, (col'd) lab, h 29 Sullivan
Davis Alvin, painter, 164 Church, h 58 College av
Davis Chancellor L, blacksmith 100 Cross, h Southport
Davis Charles, engineer, bds 1 Magee
Davis G E, engineer, bds 1 Magee
Davis George L, lawyer and justice 105 Water, h 26 William
Davis Henry, teamster, h 147 Second
Davis Henry A, h Hine nr Mt Zoar
Davis James, lab, h 99 Second
Davis James W, clerk, bds 40 Cross
Davis John, tinner, h 224 Church

DEXTER & ELMORE,

Wholesale and Retail Dealers in

Crockery, China and Glass Ware,

TABLE CUTLERY,

Kerosene, Coal Oil, & Fluid Stand & Hand Lamps,

KEROSENE AND COAL OILS,

Silver Plated Goods and Britannia Ware,

FEATHER DUSTERS,

and Manufacturers of

LOOKING-GLASSES,

ALSO, DEALERS IN

PAINTS, OILS, VARNISHES.

A Superior Quality of Varnish and Paint Brushes.
Brooklyn Premium White Lead.

Flower and Garden Seeds,

CANARY BIRDS & CAGES.

A fine assortment of GAS FIXTURES, all of which will be sold at the Lowest Prices for CASH.

GAS FITTING

Done on the shortest notice, and at the Lowest Rates at

No. 158 Water Street, Elmira, N. Y.

Davis John, shoemaker, h 40 Cross
Davis John Jr, clerk, bds 40 Cross
Davis Joseph, clerk, bds 40 Cross
Davis S, railroad agent, h 363 Water
Davis William, h 69 Gray
Davis William, (col'd) lab, h 32 Conongue
Davis William L, clerk, Haight's Hotel
Davis William R, silver plater, h 86 Church
Day Mrs C, milliner, 108 Water, h 42 High
Day William, clerk, bds 42 High
DeLabar Freeman D, carp, h 28 DeWitt
DeLancey John, engineer, h 3 S Magee
DeLancey Yates, engineer, h 3 S Magee
DeLano Daniel S, clerk, Brainard House
DeLent Thomas, ostler, C Potter
DE VOE FREDERICK A, propr "ELMIRA GAZETTE" 2 Lake, h 55 Baldwin
DeVoe Jeremiah, lab, h 64 Columbia
DeVoe Martin, boatman, bds 64 Columbia
DeWitt Abram M, grocer, 19 Baldwin, h same
DeWitt Mrs Ann, h 33 DeWitt
DeWitt Charles, billiard room, 169 Water
DeWitt Harvey, express messenger, bds Brainard House
DeWitt Ira, sup't telegraph repairs Erie R'y, bds Bevier House
DeWitt Jacob B, lab, bds 33 DeWitt
DeWitt James, peddler, bds 208 Water
DeWitt James, lawyer and justice, 4 Lake, h 3 Washington
DeWitt Peter, bds 19 Baldwin
DeWitt Miss Rachel M, tailoress, bds 33 DeWitt
DeWitt Seymour, clerk express company, bds Brainard House
DeWitt Sutherland, agt U S ex Co and Howard & Co's exp, 16 Baldwin, h 12 S Water
DeWitt Miss Ugntje, tailoress, bds 33 DeWitt
DeWitt William P, gunsmith, 83 Water, h 18 Conongue
Dean Mrs Hulda, h 18 Water
Dean Jarvis, butcher, h 232 Church
Dean John F, N Y Vol, bds 208 Water
Dean Lansing, lab, h 120 Lake
Dean Nathan L, boatman, h 108 Baldwin
Dearborn Charles, carp, bds 62 Cross
Dearborn Mark, carp, h 62 Cross
Decker David A, tanner, h 60 Clinton
Decker John, clerk, h 68 Baldwin
Decker Miss M S, dressmaker, 133 Water, h same
Decker Peter, saloon, 99 Wisner, h same
Decker Samuel, turner, h 61 First
Delam Charles A, cabinet maker, h 30 Cross
Delavan House, E O Merrill & Co prors, cor Wisner and Clinton
Delavergne Charles N, machinist, h 5 Dickinson
Delevan Richard, lab, at 78 Lake
Dempsey Bartholomew, lab, h river bank nr Hudson
Dempsey Bartholomew, shoemaker, h 37 Hudson

ELIASON, GREENER & CO.,
PIANO-FORTE MANUFACTURERS,

AND DEALERS IN ALL KINDS OF

MUSICAL MERCHANDISE,

No. 147 Water Street, Elmira, N. Y.

Pianos and Melodeons to Rent, and Rent applied if purchased.

WM. P. YATES,

DEALER IN

WATCHES, CLOCKS, JEWELRY,

Pure Silver & Plated Ware,

DENTISTS' MATERIALS,

NO. 147 WATER STREET, ELMIRA, N. Y.

Watch Repairing and Jobbing done in the best manner and Warranted.

Dempsey Dennis, lab, h Buttonwoods
Dempsey Fenton, lab, h cor Hudson and Mt Zoar
Dempsey Patrick, lab, h Hudson nr Walnut
Dempsey Timothy, lab, h 2 Washington
Dennahe Owen, lab, bds 21 DeWitt
Denniston John, spinner, h 64 Factory
Denniston Thomas C, spinner, h 58 Factory
Densmore John W, painter, h 14 Hudson
Densmore Joseph D, painter, h 10 E Second
Densmore Myron H, painter, bds 14 Hudson
Denton Mrs Ann, boarding house, 43 Main
Denton Shubael B, justice and deputy collector U S int rev, 2 Lake, h 78 Clinton
DERBY ABNER L, boots and shoes, 154 Water, h 15 S Lake
Derby Mrs Achsah R, h 26 S Water
Deryea Virgil Y, harness-maker, h 27 Hudson
Desmond John, shoemaker, h cor Main and Water
Dessauer Moses S, clerk, bds 44 Baldwin
Devine Edward, lab, h 29 Magee
Devine William, lab, h 7 Willow
Dexter Aaron, h 48 Gray
Dexter John M, (D & Elmore) h 9 College av
DEXTER & ELMORE, (John M D, Thaddeus W E) crockery etc, 158 Water
Deyster Michael, butcher, h Jay
Dias Sidney S, painter, h 7 E Union
Dick John, lab, bds cor Ann and Sly
Dick Thomas, porter, National Hotel
Dickens Miss Viann, h 33 Cross
Dickinson George S, (Barton & D) h 13 William
Dickinson Henry B, harness maker, h 95 Lake
Diester John, tanner, h 20 Jay
Diester John Jr, lab, bds 20 Jay
Diester Matthias, lab, bds 20 Jay
Diester Michael, butcher, bds 20 Jay
Diester Nicholas, lab, bds 20 Jay
Dike William, (col'd) lab, h 21 Dickinson
Dillon Gregory, shoemaker, bds 37 John
Dimon John B, lumberman, h 103 Lake
Disbrow Noah, shoemaker, h 21 Columbia
Disney Thomas, lab, bds 38 First
Diven A S & G M, (Alexander S, George M) lawyers, 153 Water
Diven Alexander S, (A S & G M D) h Horseheads rd
Diven George M, (A S & G M D) bds A S Diven, Horseheads rd
Dixon John, lab, Brainard House
Dohme John W, cigar maker, h Hudson bet S Main and Harmon
Dolan Patrick, lab, h head of Baldwin
Donald Archibald, cartman, h 8 Mt Zoar
Donohue James, lab, bds 24 Sullivan
Donohue Michael, lab, h 36 Cross
Donohue Owen, ostler, bds 21 DeWitt
Doolittle M, lab, h 24 Columbia

W. MERWIN,

Manufacturer of and Dealer in

HARNESS, SADDLES, BRIDLES,

MARTINGALES,

Trunks, Valises, Carpet Bags, &c.

No. 141 Water Street, Elmira, N. Y.

A. L. DERBY,

CASH DEALER IN

No. 154 Water-St., Elmira, N. Y.

BOOTS AND SHOES

of every style, made to order on short notice, of the
BEST MATERIAL AND WORKMANSHIP.

Doran Michael, lab, h 33 Canal
Dormaul Elias H, dry goods and millinery goods, 134 Water, boards Brainard House
Dormaul Morris, clerk, bds Haight's Hotel
Dorn Isaac L, saloon, 111 Wisner, h same
Dorr David, blacksmith, h 74 Sullivan
Dorr John, bds 74 Sullivan
Doty Charles C, photographer, 164 Water, (3 Union Block) boards Brainard House
Dounce William J, dealer in iron, 48 Fifth, h 227 Church
Dove Reuben, lab, bds 20 First
Dowling Laughlin, wines and liquors, 18 Baldwin, h 27 Fulton
Downing Daniel, N Y Vol, h 88 Gray
Doyle David T, tinner, h 37 W Union
Drake Andrew J, wagon maker, h 49 Fourth
Drake James H, railroad conductor, h 71 Davis
Drake John, painter, bds 27 Conongue
Drake Theodore M, baker, bds 7 Gray
Drury Orlando A, clerk, h 15 S Lake
DuBois Mrs F M, physician, 127 Water, h same
Duell George, tinner, bds 324 Water
Dudley George T, clerk, bds Haight's Hotel
Dudley James T, (Preswick & D) bds Brainard House
Duffy John, iron worker, Rolling Mill
Dumars R R R, capt 161 N Y Vol, h 197 Church
Dunbar Garrett R, painter, h 36 William
Duncir Lewis, shoemaker, h 28 Henry
Dundas William, sup't Elmira Woolen Manuf Co, h 26 Oak
Dunn Bernard, machinist, h 16 Columbia
Dunn D Thompson, dry-goods, groceries and crockery, 2 and 4 Lake h cor W Union and Fourth
Dunn Isaac B, bds 90 Cross
Dunn James, lawyer, h 90 Cross
Dunn James, carbuilder, h Church nr Chemung canal
Dunn John Davis, lawyer, bds 43 Main
Dunn Mrs Marilla, boarding house, 72 Water
Dunn Patrick, lab, h 16 DeWitt
Durbon Mrs H L, h 71 Gray
Durland Daniel T, (Rice, D & Pratt) bds 27 Main
Duryea Virgil Y, harness maker, h 27 Hudson
Dutcher Charles W, carp, h 2 Mt Zoar
Dyer Morgan, foundry, cor Water and Wisner, h 28 S Water
Dygart Henry, lab, h 4 Spring
Dyke William, (col'd) lab, h Dickinson

E

Eagle Hotel, T McCoy propr, 85 Wisner
Easton William H, lab, h S Water nr Harmon
Eaton Lewis, dentist, 147 Water, h 341 Water
Echenburg Friedrich, piano maker, h 83 Baldwin
Eckstein William, lab, h 33 High

JOHN I. NICKS

Manufacturer and Wholesale and Retail Dealer in

TOBACCO,  CIGARS

SNUFF, &c.,

No. 160 Water-St., Elmira, N. Y.

NO. 1 UNION BLOCK.

Orders Promptly Attended to.

Edwards Henry B, h 111 Lake
Edwards Orin, shoemaker, h 352 Water
Edwards Thomas P, carp, bds 82 Gray
Egbert ——, bridge builder, bds 1 Magee
Egbert William M, architect and builder, h 22 Columbia
Eldridge Edwin, h 2 S Main
ELIASON, GREENER & Co, (Julius E, Jacob G, Wm P Yates) glue manufs foot of John, piano manufs 160 Church, music dealers 147 Water
Eliason Julius, (E, Greener & Co) h 125 Cross
Elich Barney, pedlar, h cor DeWitt and John
Elich Moses, pedlar, h cor John and High
Elich Tobias, pedlar, h cor DeWitt and John
Elliott Mrs Ann, laundress, h 122 Baldwin
Ellis Daniel M, wagon-maker, h 20 Cross
Ellison Alanson, lab, h Horseheads rd ab Canal
Ells George, h 102 Church
Elmendorf George, painter, h Church bet Grove and Hoffman
Elmendorf William, (E & Beers) h 23 Lake
Elmendorf & Beers, (Wm E, Johnson B) restaurant, 23 Lake
ELMIRA ADVERTISER, (daily and weekly,) Seymour B Fairman pub and prop, Seymour B and Chas G Fairman editors, 8 Lake
Elmira Bank, L J Stancliff pres'dt, Wm F Corey cashier, 14 Baldwin
ELMIRA GAZETTE, (daily and weekly) Frederick A DeVoe pub and prop, Horton Tidd editor, 2 and 4 Lake
Elmira Hotel, Warner H Welch propr, 182 Water
Elmira Oil Refinery, Cook, Willis, Bedell & Co props, head of Willow nr coal basin
ELMIRA PRESS. (daily) Thayer & Whitley editors and proprs, cor Lake and Water
Elmira Rolling Mill Co. Asher Tyler pres'dt, Simeon Benjamin vice prest, Henry W Rathbone sec'y and treas, David Samuels supt, Canal nr Washington av
Elmira Savings Bank, S L Gillett sec'y and treas, 151 Church
ELMIRA STEAM MILLS, W Halliday & Co proprs, Basin
Elmira Umbrella Manufg Co, Wisner cor Fourth
Elmira Water Company, I S Hobbie pres'dt, S R VanCampen treas, Miles Ayrault supt, cor Baldwin and Water
ELMIRA WATER CURE, S O Gleason M D propr, East Hill
Elmira Woolen Manufg Co, D & R Pratt agts, Newton creek nr Factory
Elmore David, gas-fitter, h 27 Water
Elmore Devillo, hackman, h 63 Main
Elmore T O, dep'y U S Marshall, h 35 W Union
Elmore Thaddeus W, (Dexter & E) bds 27 S Water
Elore Alexander, engineer, h 58 High
Elwell John, h 71 First
Elwell John Jr, lab, bds 71 First
Elwood John C, boat builder, h Harriet nr Cross
Elwood Patrick, miller, bds Elmira & Williamsport Hotel
Ely Mrs A C, h 244 Water
Ely Edmund, nurseryman, bds S Main cor Partridge

M. RICHARDSON,

DEALER IN

Foreign & Domestic

DRY GOODS,

No. 6 Union Block,

No. 170 Water Street,

ELMIRA, N. Y.

Emmons Joseph, saloon, 91 Wisner
Enck Charls H, barber, h cor John and Conongue
Englebreck Peter, piano-maker, h 9 E Union
Ensworth Mrs Elizabeth, seamstress, h 13 Lake
Espey Daniel, iron worker, Rolling Mill
Etz John S, pedler, h 36 De Witt
Evans Jacob, cabinet maker, h 55 Gray
Evans Nathan B, (Tenny & Co) h 60 William
Evans Samuel, machinist, h Partridge nr S Main
Ewing Alexander L, clerk, bds 54 William
Ewing James, carriage manuf, cor Cross and William, h 54 William
Ewing James S, clerk, bds 54 William
Ezeski Joseph, clerk, bds Water

F

Fabian Adolph, tailor, h 65 Water
Fahr Peter, butcher, 29 E Union, h 41 Clinton
Fairman Charles G, editor ELMIRA ADVERTISER, h 5 High
FAIRMAN SEYMOUR B, pub and prop "ELMIRA ADVERTISER" 10 Lake, h 35 Hudson
FAIRMAN & DE VOE, (Seymour B F, Frederick A D) job printers and binders, 8 Lake
Falsey John, iron worker, Rolling Mill
Fancher Sutherland, (Wilson & F) h 52 Cross
Farber Jacob, lab, Haight's Hotel
Farley Christopher, lab, h 29 Clinton
Farnham George W, carriage trimmer, h 4 William
Farnham James C, billiard marker, bds 4 William
Farrar Charles S, prof Female College, h 32 Fourth
Farrell Joseph, baker, bds Chemung House
Farrington John S, grocer, h 211 Church
Farrow John, express messenger, h 68 Fifth
Fassett John, lab, h 38 Magee
Fassett Newton P, (Smith, Robertson & F) h 256 Church
Fassett Truman, livery, Cross bet Lake and Baldwin, h 32 Baldwin
Fay Cyrus W, clerk, h 306 Water
Fay Edwin G, clerk, bds 42 First
Fay Francis C, carp, bds 42 First
Fay J W, carp, h 42 First
Feeny James, gardener, at Levi J Cooley's
Feeny John, lab, h 56 High
Feeny Michael, grocer, 87 Wisner, h same
Fenderson ——, carp, bds 67 Fifth
Fennel James, lab, bds 215 Wisner
Fennel Thomas, lab, bds 215 Wisner
Fenner Benjamin P, sup't Umbrella Factory, h 52 John
Ferris Myron H, h 27 Fourth
Ferris Myron J, clerk, bds 27 Fourth
Ferris William, lab, h Willow nr Elmira Oil Refinery
Feury Dennis, lab, h 27 Jay

WILLIAM E. HART,

DEALER IN

DRY GOODS,

CARPETS,

YANKEE NOTIONS, GROCERIES, &c.

No. 110 Water Street, Elmira, N. Y.

Feury Patrick, lab, h 58 Factory
Field James, lab, h 36 Magee
Fields George W. lab, h 7 College av
Fielding John, with G H Post h 216 Church
Finch Andrew, clerk, bds Mansion House
Finch Edwin, saddler, h Broadway nr Mt Zoar
Finch Miss Lydia A, tailoress, h 4 E Union
Finley William, shoemaker, bds Elmira Hotel
Finn Luke, ostler, bds 33 William
Finn Ned. lab, h 20 First
Finnigan Thomas, pedler, h 61 High
First Methodist Church, Baldwin bet Church and Second, Rev J E Latimer, pastor
First Presbyterian Church, cor Church and Baldwin, Rev George C Curtis pastor
Fish Miss Cordelia, tailoress, h 4 East Union
Fisher Louis, brewer, h Washington av nr Canal
Fishler John V, carp, h 4 S Water
Fitch Charles, carp, h 14 Orchard
Fitch Ellery, telegraph operator, bds 64 Main
Fitch Lewis W, grocer, h 46 First
Fitch Mason P, farmer, h cor Davis and Sixth
Fitz John, lab, h 61 Wisner
Fitz Patrick, lab, h 197 Wisner
FitzGibbons ——, lab, h 199 Wisner
FitzGibbons James, iron worker, h 61 Columbia
FitzGibbons James, lab, h 28 Magee
FitzMaurice John, saloon. 55 Wisner, h same
Fitzgerald Mrs Ann, h 15 Oak
Fitzgerald David, lab, h Clinton Lane nr E Third
Fitzgerald Michael, lab, h 59 Factory
Flanagan Patrick, lab, h 30 Fourth
Fleet George, lab. at 73 Lake
Fleming Otis, h 72 William
Fleming Robert J, shoemaker h 23 Columbia
Flood Patrick Henry, physician. 44 Water, h same
Flynn Daniel, lab, bds 12 E Third
Flynn Michael, lab. h 16 Hudson
Flynn Patrick, lab, h 12 E Third
Flynn Patrick, shoemaker, h Jay
Flynn Stephen, iron worker, h 31 Canal
Flynn Thomas, lab, h 5 Washington
Foley C, iron worker, Rolling Mill
Foley Michael, lab, h 13 First
Ford Edward, clerk, bds 63 Baldwin
Ford James, shoemaker, bds 3 Gregg
Foster ——, bridge builder, bds 1 Magee
Foster Jesse, farmer, h 380 Water
Foster John, machinist, h 28 E Second
Foster Luther C, teacher, h 41 S Water
Foster Myron H, h 31 S Water
Foster William, h 375 Water

HARVEY SMITH,

(*Successor to W. H. Van Doren,*)

WHOLESALE AND RETAIL DEALER IN

CHOICE FAMILY GROCERIES

FRUITS, &c.,

No. 131 Water Street, Elmira, N. Y.

☞ Goods Delivered in any part of the City Free of Charge

U. BARTHOLOMEW,

Manufacturer, and Wholesale and Retail Dealer in

CHOICE CIGARS, TOBACCO,

PIPES, &c., &c.,

No. 9 Baldwin·St., Brainard Block, Elmira, N. Y.

W. W. ALBRO, Agent.

Fowler Daniel, lab, at 64 Water
Fowler Henry, iron worker, bds 115 Lake
Fox John, shoemaker, h 64 E Second
Fox John, cabinet maker, bds 183 Water
Fox Lewis M, music teacher and dealer in pianos and melodeons, h 343 Water
Fraly Frank, iron worker, Rolling Mill
Francer Albert, cooper, bds Wisner
Franciscoe Hiram, lab, h 20 First
Frankenstein Ellius, pedlar, h 8 Washington
Franklin House, John S Smith propr, 230 Water
Frasier Albert, clerk, bds 44 Main
Frasier F A, (F A F & Co) bds 44 Main
Frasier F A & Co, (F A F, A J Newton) druggists, American Hotel
Fredericks Daniel B, ex messenger, bds Brainard House
Freeman Charles, ex messenger, bds Delavan House
Freidman Henry, tailor, bds 87 Church
Freint John, butcher, bds 30 Water
French Asa, mason, h 35 S Water
French Benjamin R, mason, h 19 Henry
French Edson M, (Conkey & F) bds 300 Water
French George W, mason, h 118 Lake
French James A, shoemaker, h 14 Orchard
French James S, (Nelson & F) h cor Conongue and Cross
French Philip, dry goods and groceries, 171 Water, h 300 Water
French Philip, tinner, h 18 Orchard
Freundlich Henry, book-keeper, bds National Hotel
Friday William, lab, h 9 N Oak
Friedmann Frank, brick-maker, h 13 Fifth
Friedman Marcus, pedlar, h 27 Orchard
Frisbie Augustus, ex messenger, h 220 Church
Frisbie Eaton N, agt Mercur's coal yard, h 73 W Second
Frost Troilus, shoemaker, h Second av nr S Water
Fry Albert G, h 10 Oak
Fuller Daniel, carp, h 57 Columbia
Fuller Hiram, carp, h 67 Fifth
Fuller John, miller, h 262 Water
Fuller William H, shoemaker, h Fulton nr S Water
Furniss Andrew, spinner, h 68 Factory
Furey John, clerk, bds, 236 Church

G

Gabriel Benedict, carp, h 82 Clinton
Gager Miss A E, dressmaker, 145 Water, h same
Galatian And.ew B, local editor Gazette, bds 87 Second
Galatian Miss Cornelia, (Misses F & C G) h 87 Second
Galatian Miss Francis J, (Misses F & C G) h 87 Second
Galatian Misses F & C, boarding and day school for young ladies, h 87 Second
Galatian Mrs Harriet B, h 87 Second

UP STAIRS,

Nos. 5 & 6 Union Block, Water Street, Elmira,

Is My Place of Business.

I AM A PRACTICAL

Painter, Grainer, Sign-Writer & Paper-Hanger

AND "WORK AT IT."

I keep *PAINTS, OILS, VARNISHES, COLORS, GLASS, PUTTY*, and all other articles in the line, which I sell for CASH only. I employ the most experienced and practical workmen in the country, and pay them, too. I have Artists who stand at the head of their profession, exclusively for GRAINING, and others for

Sign=Writing, Curtain=Lettering, and

ORNAMENTAL PAINTING.

to all of which branches I pay particular attention. I use none but the very best materials, allow no Jobs to be slighted, whether contract or otherwise, and warrant all work satisfactory. I contract to

Paint Churches, School-Houses, Hotels,

and other Public Buildings, also private residences, large or small, furnishing Stock or otherwise, as is desired. I never ask for money on a contract till it is finished, neither do I bring in a large bill for *extras*. I pull off my coat, roll up my sleeves, and work with my men, instead of "going about seeking" to condemn other Painters' work. I am favored with a liberal patronage, and keep a large force constantly employed, still I respectfully solicit an INCREASE of BUSINESS, and will meet the demand by a proportionate increase in my number of workmen.

For reference, please apply to all who know my manner of doing business, including my *honorable* competitors.

All of which is most respectfully submitted by

WASH MARSH,
Nos. 5 and 6 Union Block, Up-Stairs.

Gallagher Timothy, street commissioner, h Wisner bet Fifth and Sixth
Gallaher, James H, architect and builder, 10 College av, h same
Gallaher Patsey, lab, bds 22 Henry
Gallavan James, lab, h Hudson bet Harmon and Fulton
Gamper John A, farmer, h Hudson nr Western limits
Gandam John, saloon, h cor Canal and Washington av
Gannan Thomas W, shoemaker, h 16 Jay
Garahy B, iron worker, Rolling Mill
Garratt William, lawyer, bds 2 Conongue
Gardiner Mrs Jane H, h 30 William
GARDINER NELSON W, hats caps and furs, 117 Water, h 308 Water
Gardiner Nicholas D, physician, 4 Lake, bds Chemung House
Garlock Edward, h Carroll nr Lake
Garr Jacob, lab, h 66 Magee
Garretson Wm C, clerk, bds 13 College av
Garritt Jacob, blacksmith, bds 100 Church
Garritt Truman, baker, h 100 Church
Garritt William L, blacksmith, bds 100 Church
Gartlan James, cooper, h 28 Jay
Gary Michael, lab, h 6 E Third
Gates Whitney, mail carrier, h 94 Cross
Gebhard Phillip A, clerk, h 7 Wisner
Geib Jacob, saloon, h 83 Wisner
Geist Joseph, painter, h Miller
George Rev A C, h 327 Water
George Henry, tailor, h 123 Water
George Henry S, carp, h 252 Water
George Lemuel, carp, h 47 Dickinson
Gerity Thomas, mason, h 81 Baldwin
German William H H, clerk, bds 26 W Union
Gerow Gardner, machinist, bds 1 W Union
Gerow Mrs Hannah, h 1 W Union
Gibbs B F, lab, bds 54 Fifth
Gibbs B R, iron worker, bds 105 Wisner
Gibbs Levi, lawyer, 105 Water, h 40 First
Gibson A Fowler, clerk, bds 69 Baldwin
Gibson Allen, millwright, h 190 Church
Gibson Mrs Georgiana, h 79 Lake
Gibson William L, 6 Ely Hall, h 69 Baldwin
Gilbert Henry S, Duncannon Iron and Nail Works Agency, 15 Canal, h 82 Lake
Gilbert Joseph C, (col'd) barber, 135 Wisner, h 17 Third
Gilbert Stephen, sash and blind maker, h 10 S Main
Gilbert William E, teacher, bds 17 William
Gilbert William F, (G & Co) bds 10 S Main
Gilbert & Co. (William F G, Hezekiah D Treadwell) boots and shoes, 125 Water
Gilday John, lab, h 4 Canal
Giles Edmund M, clerk, bds 50 Second
Giles Joseph H, carp, bds 60 High
Giles Joseph W, carp, h 60 High

ELMIRA WATER CURE.

This Cure has been open nearly eight years. Its Physicians have had a large experience in the treatment of Chronic Diseases. For more than Fifteen years they have given their best energies to the

Study and Practice of the Medical Profession.

During this time more than 10,000 cases have been prescribed for.

This Season, entirely new Bath-Rooms have been made in the Ladies' Department, equal to one room sixty feet long by sixteen wide and fitted up in good style. The increase of our business demanded better facilities, and we have spared no pains to meet the necessities and comfort of our guests.

OUR LOCATION

Has ever elicited the admiration of all our visitors and guests. It combines the bold and romantic with the more quiet and gentle phases of Nature. The city and country are at one view represented. The walks in the ravines and groves back of the Cure have been greatly improved this season. There is a new foot-bridge spanning a deep ravine—paths, with nice seats for resting places, embowered in deep shades for retreats from the scorching Summer's sun.

We do not pursue the extremes of Hydropathy or of Vegetarianism. We intend the condition of the patient shall indicate the diet and regimen necessary to promote health in each case. We seek, first of all,

TO CURE OUR PATIENTS.

WATER IS OUR CHIEF REMEDY. But we do not hesitate to use Homeopathic remedies, Electricity, or any other means within our knowledge to facilitate the recovery of the Sick. We are Eclectic in our practice—using all the means that in our judgment shall do good to any patient. Those who come to us shall have the benefit of our best skill and care.

MRS. R. B. GLEASON, M. D.,

Gives her attention to the specific treatment of the *Special Diseases of Females*. Her large experience in this department of practice—her eminent success in the cure of many who have been confined to the bed for years, entitle her to public confidence and to the large practice she has already made; having under her care all the time from thirty to sixty ladies from various States in the Union. We invite the Sick to

OUR HILL-SIDE HOME,

and pledge ourselves to do them all the good that lies within our power.

TERMS----$7.00, $7.50, $8.00, $9.00, $10.00, pr WEEK,

according to size and location of room required. Each patient is expected to furnish, for Bath purposes, 2 Comforters, 1 Blanket, 2 Sheets—linen preferred—and 6 Bath Towels. But these may be rented at the Cure.   Address   S. O. GLEASON, M. D.,
Mrs. R. B. GLEASON, M D.
Elmira, N. Y.

Gill Christopher, cigar maker, bds Chemung House
GILL BROS, (James and John) tobaconists, 198 Water
Gill James, (G Bros) bds Elmira Hotel
Gill John, (G Bros) bds 65 Lake
Gillett Solomon L, treas and sec'y Elmira Savings Bank, h 151 Church
Ginine Patrick, lab, h 5 Jay
Ginn Andrew, iron worker, h cor Fifth and Dickinson
Ginnan Daniel, lab, bds 14 Hudson
Ginnis Patrick, lab. h 207 Wisner
Givins Jesse, (G & Lindsey) h 29 College av
Givins & Lindsey, (Jesse G, Geo W L) feather renovators, 197 Water
Glabbroth August, tailor, h 119 Water
Gladke Jacob, clerk, bds 14 DeWitt
Gladke Joseph, clothing, 113 Water, h 14 DeWitt
Gladke Samuel, clerk, bds 14 DeWitt
Gladiator Silas (col'd) lab, h 36 Cross
Glancy Thomas, lab, bds 6 S Lake
Gleason James, lab, h Beach nr Factory
Gleason Mrs R B, physician, Elmira Water Cure
GLEASON SILAS O, propr Elmira Water Cure, East Hill
Gline John, butcher, h 9 Hudson
Goddard Edward, lab, bds 64 College av
Goddard John, N Y Vol, h 64 College av
Goddard Levi, shoemaker, h 64 College av
Goddard Samuel, brakeman, bds 64 College av
Godfrey John H, umbrella maker, bds 1 Magee
Goeings Joseph, (col'd) lab. h Franklin nr S Main
Gohring George E, tailor, h 15 S Water
Goines George F, (col'd) porter, Brainard House
Goldsmith Benjamin, grocer, 55 Water, h 59 Water
Goldsmith Mrs Margaret, h 17 Water
Goldsmith Mrs Sarah, tailoress, h 77 Sullivan
Goodell DeBruce, machinist, h 31 Wisner.
Goodman William F. (col'd) physician, 52 Lake, h 15 E Fifth
Goodrich Chauncey S, blacksmith, h 60 Gray
Goodrich Dwight A, clerk, bds 40 First
Goodrich John, clerk, bds 40 First
Goodrich John R, (Carpenter, Perry & Co) and clerk Brainard House, bds Brainard House
Goodwin Frances, lab, h 4 Canal
Goosler John A, cloth shearer, h 2 Clinton
Gorman Dennis, grocer, 113 Wisner h 69 Second
Gorman Edward, grocer, h 50 Magee
Gorman John, clerk, bds 69 Second
Gorman John, lab, h Wisner bet Fifth and Sixth
Gorman Martin, lab, h 24 Perry
Gorman Patrick, grocer, Wisner nr Fifth,' h same
Gorman Simon, iron worker, Rolling Mill
Goslin Thomas, bridge builder, bds 1 Magee
Gosper E, clerk, bds 8 S Main
Gosler John A, lab, h 2 Clinton
Gother James, (col') lab, h 28 Dickinson

EYE & EAR INFIRMARY.

DR. UP DE GRAFF,
Oculist, Aurist & General Surgeon,
ELMIRA, N. Y.

Treats all Diseases of the Eye, Ear and Throat.

THE EYE.

He will operate upon Cataract, Artificial Pupil, Cross Eyes, Lachrymal Fistula, Pterygium, Entropion, (inversion of the eyelid,) and treat all forms of "SORE EYES," such as Granulated Lids, Purulent Opthalmia, Opacities of the Cornea, Scrofulous diseases of the Eye, and all diseases to which the Eye is subject.

THE EAR.

Treats successfully Discharges from the Ear, Noises in the Ear, Difficulty of Hearing, Deafness, (even when the *drum* is entirely destroyed, will insert an artificial one, answering nearly all the purposes of the natural.)

THE THROAT,

Ulcerated Throat, Enlarged Tonsils, *Catarrh* of the Throat and Nose; causing hardness of hearing—permanently cured.

GENERAL SURGERY.

He will operate upon Club Feet, Hair Lip, Cleft Palate, Tumors, Cancers, Morbid Growths, Deformities from Burns, Contracted Limbs, &c., and performs

PLASTIC OPERATIONS.

Where the Nose, Lips, or any portion of the face is destroyed through disease or otherwise, by healing them on anew. Will attend to the Amputation of Limbs, and General Surgery in all its branches.

INSERTS ARTIFICIAL EYES,

Giving them all the motion and expression of the natural, defying detection. They are inserted without removing the old one, or producing pain.

The Doctor's collection of Instruments comprises all the latest improvements, and is the largest in the State. The superior advantages he has had in perfecting himself in all that is new and valuable in Surgery, warrants him in saying that everything within the bounds of the profession may be expected of him.

Patients from a distance can be accommodated with boarding on reasonable terms.

Office in River Buildings, opposite the Brainard House, ELMIRA, N. Y.

Goulden Joseph, cabinet maker, h 50 High
Grace James, lab, at Elmira Hotel
Grace Patrick, lab, h 27 Water
Grady Michael, lab, h 63 Wisner
Grady Michael, lab, h 205 Wisner
Grady Thomas, lab, h 15 First
Grand Morris, clerk, bds 28 High
Granger Samuel, carp, h 30 DeWitt
Grant John P, blacksmith, h 24 E Second
Gray Charles, (col'd) lab, h 18 Perry
Gray Guy H, produce dealer, h 325 Water
Gray P Wells, homeopathic physician, 8 Ely Hall, h 250 Water
Greatsinger Christian, h 22 Conongue
Green Benjamin, (col'd) lab, h Second av nr S Water
Green Abram, saloon, 197 Water, h same
Green Elnathan J, carp, h 52 Gray
Green Isaac S, music teacher, bds 22 E Second
Green Mrs Jane, tailoress, h 123 Baldwin
Greene Mrs Kate, h 74 Church
Greener Jacob, (Eliason, G & Co) h 160 Church
Gregg John H, h 6 Conongue
Gregg John W, clerk, h 78 John
Gregg William M, Major 23 N Y Vol, h 57 Sullivan
Gregory George W, mason, h 82 Gray
Gregory Hiram, cartman, h 145 Second
Greves John, clerk, bds 64 Main
Gridley Grandison A, (G & Davenport) h 3 S Water
GRIDLEY & DAVENPORT, (Grandison A G, Ephraim D) hardware 109 Water
Griffin Mrs ——, h 73 Wisner
Griffin Bradley, lumberman, h 211 Church
Griffin Mrs Jane, h 97 Cross
Griffin Thomas, iron worker, Rolling Mill
Griffith Fleming, barkeeper, Haight's Hotel
Griggs George W, carp, h 91 First
Guernsey Ira B, bridge builder, h 42 Main
Gunn George D, cigar maker, bds 6 Fox
Gunn Stephen J, cigar maker, h 6 Fox
Gunnison Christopher, carp, h 72 Columbia
Guttenberg Marx, (G, Rosenbaum & Co) res New York City
Guttenberg, Rosenbaum & Co, (Marx G, Leman R, Louis Holzheimer) clothing, 162 Water

H

Haase Henry, grocer and butcher, 105 Church, h same
Hackett Mrs Mary Ann, h 74 Church
Hackett Patrick, painter, h Sly's Plot
Hackley H D, tinner, h 37 Wisner
Hackley Henry, clerk, h 93 Cross
Hadley J J, shoemaker, bds 93 Cross

Hagadorn Charles, clerk, bds 49 Baldwin
Haight Leonard, leather dealer, h 6 Main
Haight's Hotel, cor Cross and Lake, William T Reeder propr
Hall Augustus, lab, bds 11 Fifth
Hall Charles C, (H Bros) bds 27 Main
HALL BROTHERS, (Frederic, Charles C, Robert A) booksellers &c, 128 Water
Hall Francis G, bookkeeper, bds 73 Lake
Hall Frederic, (H Bros) h 17 College av
Hall John, machinist, bds 11 Fifth
Hall Robert A, (H Bros) bds 17 College av
Hall Samuel, h junction Oak and Lake
Hall Mrs Temperance, h 11 Fifth
Halliday Freeman B, grocer, h 50 Gray
Halliday Samuel I, physician, h 206 Water
Halliday Smith, lab, h 42 Gray
HALLIDAY W & CO, (William H, Edgar C Merrill) proprs Elmira Steam Mills, Basin
Halliday William, (W H & Co) and Sheriff Chemung County, Court House, h 62 Lake
Halliday William, mason, h 4 Grove
Halloran Martin, lab, h 8 E Third
Halloran Patrick, lab, at 76 Water
Hamer Wm F, cutter S G Stryker, h 24 Dewitt
HAMILTON CHARLES, saloon, 173 Water, h same
Hamilton Daniel S, watch maker and jeweller, 36 Carroll, h 10 Fox
Hamilton Frederick, watch maker, bds 10 Fox
Hamilton George W, wagon maker, bds 10 Fox
Hamilton Mrs Mary A, (col'd) laundress, h 4 Perry
Hamilton Oliver, shingle maker, h 74 Baldwin
Hamilton Walter, tinner 36 Lake, h 33 Water
Hamlin Samuel S, h 73 Lake
Hanan Mathew, cartman, h 46 College av
Hanan Michael, lab, h 63 Gray
Hanson William, carp, bds 60 College av
Hancock Benjamin F, tinner, h 53 Cross
Handoran John, teamster, h 60 Factory
Hankins Zackery T, carp, h 72 Clinton
Hardy James H, lawyer, 103 Water, h 24 Jay
Harley Charles, iron worker, bds cor Willow and Washington av
Harper Joseph, switch tender, h 7 West Third
Harrington B, lab, h cor John & Harriet
Harris Joseph, h 344 Water
Harris Monroe, pedlar, h 62 Gray
Harrop James, iron worker, h Willow
Harsh William, umbrella maker, h cor Third and Perry
HART ABRAHAM P, photographer, 22 Lake, h 38 Factory
Hart Charles L, clerk, bds 78 Lake
Hart Erastus L, physician, 78 Lake, h same
Hart Erastus P, lawyer, 15 Lake, bds Brainard House
Hart Ira F, physician, 147 Church, h same

Hart Jacob, shoemaker, h 51 William
Hart Solomon, baker, h 1 College av
HART WILLIAM E, dry goods, carpets and groceries, 110 Water, h 29 Gray
Haskell Edward, turner, h 4 Grove
Haskell Erastus, (H & Bro) h 102 College av
Haskell Henry T, boatman, h 51 William
Haskell Perez, (H & Bro) h 102 College av
HASKELL WILLIAM H, dry goods, 7 Baldwin, bds Brainard House
Haskell & Bro, (Perez and Erastus) coal dealers, 14 Gray
Hassett John, lab, h Seventh bet Hatch and Canal
Hatch Dorus, carp, h 26 Main
Hatch Harry, millwright, h 28 Gray
Hatch William B, upholsterer, h 53 Cross
Hatch William S, dealer in lumber and coal, h 39 Main
Hathaway Samuel G Jr, (H & Woods) Col 141st N Y Vol, bds Haight's Hotel
Hathaway & Woods, (Samuel G H Jr, James L W) lawyers, 151 Water
Hathorn Andrew, h 35 W Union
Hauenstein Heinrich, butcher, 32 Lake, h 83 Cross
Haupt Andrew, tailor, h 3 DeWitt
Haupt Henry, tailor, h 75 John
Haupt Matthew, tailor, h 75 John
Haviland Addison T, machinist, h 4 Hudson
Haviland Mrs Anna, h 47 W Second
Haviland George L, tinner, h 25 Gray
Haviland James, lawyer, bds 47 W Second
Hawkins Mrs Anna, h 65 Cross
Hawkins Mrs Bridget, h cor High and Jay
Hawley Charles, iron worker, Rolling Mill
Hawley Robert E, clerk, American Hotel
Haynes Sanford, harness maker, bds Chemung House
Hayes Sylvester, lab, h cor Broadway and Fulton
Hazard Charles, printer, bds 27 First
Hazard Josiah, clerk, bds 26 First
Hazard Louis A, N Y Vol, bds 27 First
Haze James, lab, h Walnut nr Hudson
Hazelton Charles A, blacksmith, bds 93 Cross
Heffron Thomas, lab at 96 Lake
Hefner Patrick, waiter, Brainard House
Hellis William, lab, h 47 Washington
Helmes ——, shoemaker, bds 6 S Lake
Helmes Morris, watchman, h Clinton bet College av and Columbia
Helmes Samuel, shoemaker, h 21 S Water
Hemenway Andrew J, R R baggage master, h 26 Henry
Hemenway Charles W, clerk, bds 4 Henry
Hemenway Seth, lab, h 3 Clinton
Hemenway William W, carp, h 4 Henry
Hemingway Miss Anna M, clerk, bds 13 Henry
Hemingway George, lab, h Clinton
Hendrick Burr, clerk, h 120 Cross

R. WATROUS,

DEALER IN

HARDWARE & CUTLERY,

IRON, STEEL, NAILS,

PAINTS, OILS & GLASS,

Carriage & Saddlery Hardware,

BELTING, &c.

Sign of the Padlock, No. 112 Water Street,

ELMIRA, N. Y.

Hendrickson ——, bridge builder, bds 1 Magee
Hendy John, bds 3 Ann
Hennessey John, lab, h 11 Washington
Henry Barney, lab, h 18 First
Henry James, lab, h Hatch
Hepburn Albert H, R R conductor, bds Brainard House
Hepinstall Richard, tanner, h Harmon bet S Water and Hudson
Hermans Rev Edwin J, pastor Hedding Church, h 212 Church
Hern Thomas, lab, h 129 Lake
Heron James, physician, h 2 E Union
Herrick Benjamin F, (H & Snyder) h 22 DeWitt
Herrick & Snyder, (Benjamin F H, Geo W S) carriage manufs, cor Cross and Fox
Hersey Edward W, (J H Loring & Co) h 119 Cross
Hewitt Gurdeon Jr, 5 Lake, bds 144 Church
Hewener Jacob, (Kellogg & H) bds 63 Baldwin
Hibbard Solon A, carp, h 339 Water
Hibler Louisa, seamstress, h 60 Main
Hickcock E, brakeman, bds 1 Magee
Hickey Martin, lab, h 28 Henry
Hickok Sereno, quarryman, h 13 Henry
Higgins Elisha, blacksmith, bds 223 Church
Higgins James, lab, h 92 Baldwin
Higgins Norman L, blacksmith, 3 Carroll h 223 Church
Higgins Patrick, tailor, h 19 Orchard
Hill Charles J, (col'd) barber, Haight's Hotel, h 34 Dickinson
Hill James W, chief of police, h 7 Wisner
Hill M, carpenter, bds 60 College av
Hill Robert N, wagon maker, h 21 Conongue
Hilton Jacob, lab, h 4 E Third
Hilton William R, lab, bds 4 E Third
Hinckley ——, freight agent, h 33 W Union
Hine Jay S, farmer, h cor Hine and Mt Zoar
Hines Oscar O, printer and painter, h 79 Water
Hines William A, dentist, 133 Water, h Grove nr Sixth
Hison George, shoemaker, bds 93 Cross
Hison William, pedlar, bds 60 S Water
Hitchcock Albert T, clerk, bds 16 S Lake
Hitchcock Harmon, (H & Loomis) h 16 S Lake
Hitchcock & Loomis, (Harmon H and William R) butchers, 39 Lake
Hoats Jonas, blacksmith, bds 3 Conongue
Hochstetter George, (L Straus & Co) bds Brainard House
Hockenberger William, lime kiln, canal bank nr Washington av, h Washington av
Hoffman George, farmer, h 86 Hoffman
Hoffman H C, Col 23d N Y Vol, bds 336 Water
Hoffman Henry, (Brand & H) res South America
Hoffman John S, farmer, h 326 Water
Hoffman Peter, lab, at foot of Church
Hoffman Miss Susan A, dressmaker, h 113 Lake
Hoffman William, farmer, h 336 Water
Hogan Anthony, lab, h 26 Perry

THOMAS BURNS,

DEALER IN

GROCERIES & PROVISIONS,

FLOUR & FEED,

Fruit, &c.,

No. 95 Water-St., Elmira, N. Y.

R. MORRIS,

DEALER IN

GROCERIES, PROVISIONS,

FLOUR, FEED,

BUTTER, CHEESE, LARD, PORK, FISH,

&c., &c., &c.,

No. 5 Lake Street, Elmira. N. Y.

Hogan Dennis, lab, h 213 Wisner
Hogg John, tanner, h bet High and E Third
Holbert Thomas, teacher, h 59 First
Holden Delos L, bds F Holden
Holden Fox, h Holden's Hall
Holden Lyman J, clerk, bds 72 Water
Holdridge Harrison, nursery. h Fulton nr Franklin
Holland Alfred, (col'd) lab, h 43 Dickinson
Holland Anthony D, clerk, bds 13 S Water.
Holland Thomas, lab, h 55 Dickinson
Holland William, h 13 S Water
Hollenbeck Mrs Elizabeth M, laundress, h 45 Clinton
Holley Mrs Martha, h 10 S Lake
Holmes E F, bds 40 Main
Holmes Humphrey H, h 63 College av
Holmes William, (col'd) lab, h 34 Conongue
Holzheimer Louis, (Guttenberg, Rosenbaum & Co) h 156 Church
Hooton William, machinist, h 13 E Union
Hopkins Merchant, lab, h 10 S Lake
Hoppe Charles, barber, 131 Water, h same
Horricks Joshua, weaver, bds 24 Oak
Horton Byron C, manuf grain cleaners, bds 118 Cross
Horton Chase B, manuf Horton's grain cleaners, h 118 Cross
Hotchkin Samuel, Elmira Mills, Water nr College av, res West of Village
Hotchkiss Thomas W, produce dealer, h 298 Water
Houston Charles P, with C E Wells, bds 324 Water
Howard Dennis, saloon, 55 Wisner, h same
Howard James, lab, h 203 Wisner
Howard & Co's Express, Sutherland DeWitt agt, 16 Baldwin
Howell John, engineer, h 84 Second
Howes Ephraim W, liquor dealer, 9 Fox, bds 89 Church
Howes Orson, distiller, h 35 Water
Howes Mrs Sarah, milliner, 104 Water, h 35 Water
Howland Gaylord, blacksmith, h 35 Orchard
Howland James B, carp, h Franklin nr Fulton
Howland Mrs Lucretia, h 7 Jay
Howland Ozial H, carp, h 26 Jay
Hoyt ——, carp, bds 67 Fifth
Hoyt Charles, N Y Vol, bds 14 Gray
Hoyt Norman F, N Y Vol, bds 14 Gray
Hoyt William, carp, h 14 Gray
Hubbard Samuel L, meat market, h 115 Cross
HUBBELL SAMUEL B, furniture, looking-glasses, &c, 174 Water, h 41 First

Hudson George W, painter, h 125 Lake
Hudson Mrs Harriet, h 26 S Lake
Huggard William G, carp, h 46 Fourth
Hughes George, boatman, h 51 Water
Hughes Miss Helen A, h 23 High
Hughes Isaac, lab, bds 46 Oak
Hughes John, blacksmith, h 44 Oak

J. M. TILLMAN,

Manufacturer of and Dealer in

Harness, Saddles, Bridles & Whips,

No. 41 Lake Street,

ELMIRA, N. Y.

MAURICE LEVY,

Manufacturer of and Dealer in

TOBACCO, SNUFF AND CIGARS,

German and French Clay and China Pipes,

MEERSCHAUM PIPES AND CIGAR TUBES,

WHOLESALE & RETAIL,

No. 33 Lake Street, Elmira, N. Y.

H. W. M'INTIRE,

MANUFACTURER OF

Shingle Machines,

(JOHNSON'S IMPROVED PATENT.)

No. 12 Wisner St., Elmira, N. Y.

GILL BROS,

Manufacturers of and Wholesale & Retail Dealers in

TOBACCO, CIGARS, & SNUFF,

German & French Clay, & China & Meerschaum Pipes,

And every Article usually found in a first class Tobacco Establishment.

No. 198 Water Street, Elmira, N. Y.

JAMES GILL.   JOHN GILL.

Hughes John, lab, h 6 Hatch
Hughes Miss Sarah H, bds 23 High
Hughes Thomas, lab, h Tuthill av, nr Church
Hughes Thomas, lab, h 46 Oak
Hulbert George, carp, h 127 Lake
Hull Rev Andrew, Rector Trinity Church, h 22 Main
Hull George H, carp, h 74 Cross
Hulligan William, carp, at 12 Wisner
Hulse Mrs Ceceilia, h 13 S Lake
Humphrey George W, florist, 20 E Second, h same
Humphrey John, cabinet maker, h 20 E Second
Humphrey Lucius A, clerk, bds 13 High
Hunt Franklin K, tanner, h 14 College av
Hunt James, lab, h 98 Gray
Hunt Thomas, whip and glove maker, 191 Water, h 5 Mt Zoar
Hunt William G, barber, National Hotel, h 4 College av
Hunter Myron A, plaster grinder, h Tuthill av, nr Water
Huntley Elias S, (H & Cole) h 80 Baldwin
Huntley George R, boatbuilder, h 27 Orchard
Huntley I, lab, h Clinton, nr Davis
Huntley & Cole, (Elias S H, Myron C) grocers, 129 Water
Hurd Norman, h 245 Church
Hurlburt Luman D, constable, h 12 Gray
Hurley Lawrence, lab, h cor Hudson and Lawrence
Huston James C, printer, h 24 S Water
Hutchins John, (H & Co) h 221 Church
Hutchins & Co, (John H, Josiah C Simons) grocers, 218 Water
Hutchinson Edwin P, bookkeeper, h 25 W Union
Hutchinson Mrs Eliza, h 16 Orchard
HUTCHINSON SAMUEL S, boots and shoes, 126 Water, house 10 Columbia
Hylen Robert F, h 70 Baldwin
Hylen William L, clerk, bds 70 Baldwin

I

Ingraham Clark S, (Robinson & I) bds 92 Cross
Innis Patrick, lab, h 211 Wisner

J

Jackson John, (col'd) lab, h 19 Dickinson
Jackson John S, painter, h 55 William
Jacobs Charles, (col'd) lab, h Franklin nr Fulton
Jacobs Julius, clothier, 127 Water, h 65 Cross
Jadwin Joseph, tanner, h 11 S Water
James William, carp, h 57 Gray
James William H, (col'd) lab, h 16 Perry
James Richard, lab, h 30 Oak
Jeffers William M, planing mill, 85 Baldwin, h 57 William

Jenkins Edward S, machinist, h 30 Hudson
Jenkins Mrs Helena C, h 21 Columbia
Jenks George W, shingle maker, bds 1 Magee
Jenks Mrs Mary Jane, h 341 Water
Jervis Joel S, teamster, h 56 Washington
Jessop Nicholas, lab, h 2 Clinton
Jewett Thomas M, h 64 William
Jewett Thomas M Jr, (Bliven & J) h 69 College av
Jilson Samuel C, railroad conductor, h 78 Second
Johnson Mrs Catharine L, boarding house, 27 Conongue
Johnson George, lab, h Fulton bet Hudson and River
Johnson George H, boatman, bds 7 Ann
Johnson Isaac L, lab, h 20 Wisner
Johnson John, tailor, h 27 Orchard
Johnson John C, boatman, h 7 Ann
Johnson John H, blacksmith, h Horseheads rd ab Canal
Johnson Samuel, (col'd) lab, h 16 Dickinson
Johnson Thomas, watchmaker and jeweller, 22 Carroll, bds Haight's Hotel
Johnson Welcome, carp, h 99 Church
Johnson William, carp, h 26 Fourth
Johnson William, lab, h 88 Second
Johnson William, (col'd) lab, bds 121 Lake
Johnson William, (col'd) h 23 Dickinson
Johnson Willard L, carp, bds 99 Church
Jones Elijah, h 68 Clinton
Jones Miss Elizabeth, dressmaker, bds 10 E Second
Jones George W, (col'd) lab, h 15 Third
Jones John R, (J R J & Co) h S Lake
Jones John R & Co, (J R J, Richmond Jones) com merchants, 100 Water
Jones John W, (col'd) lab, h 185 Church
JONES JOSHUA, prop "Arbour" 7, 9 and 11 Lake, h same
Jones Richmond, (J R J & Co) h 62 Clinton
Jones Samuel T, h 47 William
Jones William D, iron worker, h bet Willow and RR
Jones William M, mason, h 131 Lake
Jordan James, stone mason, h 30 Orchard
Josse Miss Mina, dressmaker, cor Lake and Water
Judd Theodorus, h 1 Columbia
Judson William, lumber dealer, h 36 Second

K

Kain James, bridge builder, h 12 Hatch
Kanady J, h Wisner bet Church and First
Kane Mrs, dressmaker, h 81 Wisner
Kane Cornelius, lab, h 6 Spring
Kane Dennis, blacksmith, bds 83 Church
Kane Mrs Mary, h 13 Jay
Kane Morris, lab, h 8 Washington

Kane Patrick, blacksmith, h 15 Sullivan
Karst Adam, lab, bds 13 Fifth
Kavanaugh John, cartman, h 14 Hatch
Kavanagh Rev Martin, h 66 Cross
Keanneard George W, carp, h 4 Ann
Keefe Patrick, lab, h Sly's Plot
Keiffe James, lab, h Hatch
Keiffe Patrick, lab, h 52 College av
Kellogg Eli A, lumberman, h 10 E Second
Kellogg Lovell, (K & Hevener) h 62 William
Kellogg Seth W, painter, h 87 Gray
Kellogg Wesley W, h 117 Cross
Kellogg William W, agent Barclay Coal Co, junction Chemung and Penn Canal, h 117 Cross
Kellogg & Hevener, (Lovell K, Jacob H) druggists &c, 133 Water
Kelly, Biggs & Co, (Seth K, Peter B, H Sayles) tallow chandlers, 34 Fifth
Kelly George, shoemaker, bds 22 E Second
Kelly George H, painter, bds 22 E Second
Kelly James, baker, bds Mansion House
Kelly John, lab, h 35 Canal
Kelly John, shoemaker, bds Elmira Hotel
Kelly Martin, iron worker, bds 20 First
Kelly Michael, lab, h 16 Washington
Kelly Michael, brakeman, bds Mansion House
Kelly Seth, (K, Biggs & Co) h 116 Cross
Kelly William D, shoemaker, h 22 E Second
Kelsey George W, clerk, bds Delavan House
Kemmery Adam, iron worker, h 63 Washington av
Kennedy Allen A, contractor, h 59 William
Kennedy Charles H, iron worker, h 21 Fifth
Kennedy David, boatbuilder, h 111 Baldwin
Kennedy John, shoemaker, bds 206 Water
Kennedy Oliver C, h 8 W Third
Kent Phineas L, painter, h 95 First
Keough John, saloon, 53 Wisner, h same
Keough Michael, saloon, 57 Wisner, h same
Keyser Tobias H, shoemaker, bds 347 Water
Keyser William, shoemaker, h 347 Water
Kies Louis, bookbinder, with Fairman & DeVoe, h 47 Gray
Kikbush John M, tailor, h 42 High
King Enos, shoemaker, h 12 S Lake
King Henry, hackman, bds 66 College av
King John, (col'd) lab, h 32 Dickinson
King Rufus, lawyer, 137 Water, bds 27 Main
King Simeon, lab, h First nr Wisner
King Theron, harness maker, h 176 Church
King William, hackman, bds 66 College av
Kingman William M, clerk, bds 27 Main
Kingsbery Henry, clerk, h 161 Water
Kingsbery Mrs M, milliner, 161 Water, h same
Kingsbury Elisha, carp, h 73 College av

E. COVELL & CO.,

DEALERS IN

DRY GOODS,

GROCERIES,

BOOTS & SHOES,

No. 106 Water Street, Elmira, N. Y.

We buy all kinds of Country Produce and pay the highest market price in CASH.

Kingsbury Oliver C, meat market, h 5 Columbia
Kingsbury William A, grocer, 222 Water, h 122 Cross
Kingsley Andrew, wagon maker, h 30 E Second
Kingsley Thomas, gardener, h Hudson bet Harmon and Fulton
Kingsley William C, lawyer, with Hathaway & Woods, bds 12 Main
Kinner John V, engineer, h 40 College av
Kinney James A, blacksmith, bds 3 Conongue
Kinney Thomas, lab, h Elm nr S Lake
Kirk William G, carp, h 13 Jay
Kirkland James, painter, h 15 Gregg
Kline John, butcher, h Southport
Klock Monroe, mason, bds 61 Factory
Klock Peter S, mason, bds 61 Factory
Klock Sanford, mason, h 61 Factory
Koch Charles, clerk, at David R Reubens
Kolb Baldwin, Exchange Hotel, 139 Wisner, h same
Konkle Mrs Mary, h cor High and Cross
Knapp George A, clerk, h 70 William
Knapp John S, policeman, h Fifth nr College av
Knapp John M, clerk, h 45 Main
Knapp William B, harness maker, 75 Water, h 11 High
Kniffin Daniel D, Lieut N Y Vol, h 30 Hudson
Knipp John, confectioner, bds 93 Water
Kniskern James, Mansion House, cor Second and Wisner
Knott Alvin A, milkman, h 29 High
Knott Robert H, carp, h 29 High
Knowland John, clerk, bds 69 Second
Knowles M M, hackman, h 38 College av
Kraiger Emmett, railroad baggageman, bds 4 William
Kreager G J, bridge builder, bds 1 Magee
Kress Benjamin, h 95 Church
Kress George, oil inspector, h 41 Cross
Kress Jacob, bds 41 Cross
Kromer William, lab, h 125 Baldwin
Kromer William Jr, iron worker, h 53 Dickinson
Krowl Abraham, blacksmith, 38 Lake, h 14 High

L

LaBuskie Francis, tailor, h 20 Perry
LaDue Freeman, cooper, bds 21 Cross
LaDue Hiram W, cooper, h 21 Cross
LaDue Jeremiah H, carp, h First nr Chemung Canal
LaFrance Lemuel, jeweler, bds cor Cross and Harriet
LaFrance Peter A, agt furniture, 159 Water, h Hudson bet S Main and Harmon
LaFrance Truckson S, engineer, h 36 Harriet
LaFrance Willis B, carp, h 36 Harriet
LaMont Miss Emma, teacher, bds 63 Baldwin
Labar Robert, drayman, bds 206 Church
Laffin Philip, teamster, h 33 Clinton

Collingwood Brothers,

DEALERS IN

WATCHES, CLOCKS, JEWELRY, SILVER-WARE,

&C., &C., &C.,

AGENTS FOR

SINGER'S SEWING MACHINES,

Twist, Cotton, Oil and Needles, for Grover & Baker's, Wheeler & Wilson's, Ladd & Webster's, Finkle & Lyon's, and all other principal styles of Sewing Machines.

No. 13 Lake Street, Elmira, N. Y.

REPAIRING OF ALL KINDS DONE.

Baldwin & Reynolds,

MERCHANT TAILORS.

DEALERS IN

Cloths, Cassimeres, Vestings, Gents' Furnishing Goods,

READY-MADE CLOTHING,

Military Uniforms Made on Short Notice,

No. 149 Water-St.,....Opposite the Brainard House,

THOS. D. BALDWIN,
S. N. REYNOLDS,
}   ELMIRA, N. Y.

Laidlaw John, shoemaker, h 331 Water
Laidlaw John F, plumber, h 6 Hudson
Lambert Mathew, carp, h 81 Sullivan
Lamphier Ambrose, tobacconist, bds National Hotel
Landers Garrett, tailor, h Hudson bet Harmon and Fulton
Landy Peter, agt Ink manuf, h 11 Henry
Langdon J & Co, (Jervis L, S W Barnard) coal dealers, 46 Fifth
Langdon Jervis, (J L & Co) h 21 Main
Langford James, carp, bds 2 Conongue
Lantry Mrs Caroline, h 13 S Lake
Lariew Almeron, painter, h 18 E Second
Larkin Mrs Bridget, h 8 Spring
Larkin J Edward, artist, bds 21 William
Larkin Mathew, cigar maker, bds 8 Spring
Larkins Robert, cartman, h 70 Second
Larkins Thomas, lab, at 28 William
Latimer David, lab, h 34 DeWitt
Latimer James, lab, h cor High and Jay
Latimer Rev James E, Pastor First Methodist Church, h 45 Baldwin
Lawrence Abram, carp, h 85 Second
Lawrence J Ricketts, h 77 Main
Lawrence Richard H, bds cor High and Cross
Lawrence William H, Capt U S A, bds Haight's Hotel
Laws Benjamin, (col'd) lab, h 24 Fifth
Leach Eugene, bar keeper, bds 90 Second
Leach George, clerk, bds 90 Second
Leach Richard, clerk, h 90 Second
Leach Robert, lab, bds 90 Second
Leary Bartholomew, cigar maker, bds 3 E Third
Leary Cornelius, lab, h 37 Canal
Leary Dennis, lab, h nr Hudson
Leary Fenton, lab, h Walnut nr Hudson
Leary John, lab, bds 3 E Third
Leary Mrs Mary, h cor Hudson and Fulton
Leary Patrick, baggageman, h Wisner nr Fifth
Leary Patrick, cigar maker, bds 3 E Third
Leary Thomas, lab, h 3 E Third
Leavitt Charles, clerk, bds 5 College av
Leavitt Henry C, machinist, h 5 College av
Leavitt John H, storekeeper U S Disbursing Office, bds 94 Cross
Leavitt Milton T, engineer, h 11 Fox
Ledbeter Samuel M, machinist, h 43 Oak
Lee Arthur T, Major U S A, bds Haight's Hotel
Lee George, bar keeper, American Hotel
Lee James, bds Haight's Hotel
Lee John P, (col'd) lab, bds 27 Dickinson
Lee Joshua, (col'd) teamster, h 12 Perry
Lee Thomas, (col'd) grocer, 51 Wisner, h same
Lee Thomas J, physician, 22 Henry, h same
Lee William, policeman, 26 Baldwin, h same
LEHMAN E & CO, (Elias L, Gustavus Rice) mer tailors, 151 Water
Lehman Elias, (E L & Co) bds Brainard House

JOHN D. COVELL,
DRUGGIST,
AND DEALER IN

Paints, Oils, Dye-Stuffs, Patent Medicines,

PERFUMERY, BRUSHES,

AND DRUGGISTS FANCY ARTICLES GENERALLY.

KEROSENE OIL, CAMPHENE & BURNING FLUID.

No. 102 Water St., Elmira, N. Y.

Physicians Prescriptions Carefully Prepared.

E. B. SMITH,

WHOLESALE & RETAIL DEALER IN

CONFECTIONERY,

BREAD, CRACKERS, CAKES, &C.

An Extensive Stock of Toys always on Hand.

No. 1 Brainard Block, Water Street, Elmira, N. Y.

Orders Filled for Parties or Weddings on Short Notice.

Lehnseitren Marcus, lab, h Beach nr Factory
Leibby Gotleib, iron worker, Rolling Mill
Leinhart Andrew, saloon, 95 Wisner, h same
Lenhart Oliver, iron worker, h Washington av
Lennahan James, iron worker, Rolling Mill
Lennox James, iron worker, h 133 Lake
Lessey Prosper C W, shoemaker, h 195 Water
Letterman George, cigar maker, h 13 Orchard
LEVY MAURICE, tobacconist, 33 Lake, h 37 Water
Lewis Arnold, lab, h 219 Church
Lewis Edward P, railroad ticket agent, h 11 Gray
Lewis George E, N Y Vol, h 217 Church
Lewis Henry, mason, h 26 Washington
Lewis Isaac, clerk, bds 56 Water
Lewis John L, carp, h 238 Church
Liddle William, iron worker, Rolling Mill
Liddy Jeremiah, h S Lake nr Miller
Liddy Patrick, lab, h Washington av nr Chemung Canal
Lincoln P B, carp, bds Bevier House
Lincoln Rev T O, Pastor First Baptist Church, h 26 College av
Linderman Ira M, blacksmith, h 6 High
Lindsey George W, (Givins & L) bds 29 College av
Lindsey William, bridge builder, bds 1 Magee
Linehan James, iron worker, bds 115 Lake
Lisdell David, lab, h 26 Third
Little William, lab, h 5 W Union
Livingston Theola, shoemaker, Bigelow & Richardson
Lobdell Isaac, mason, h 31 Orchard
Locke Hiram B, lab, h 68 Second
Lockwood Mrs Ann, h 54 S Water
Lockwood Gideon, cartman, h 51 Cross
Lockwood John, carp, h 45 Clinton
Loggie John, engineer, h 64 Second
Loggie John Jr, fireman, bds 64 Second
Lohman Henry, boat builder, h 22 Fifth
Lombard Horatio J, propr National Hotel, 24 Baldwin
Long Charles, lab, bds 40 Oak
Long Mrs Nancy, h 40 Oak
Loomis William R, (Hitchcock & L) bds 17 S Lake
Loop Christian, lab, h 46 Sullivan
Loop George, moulder, h 11 Fox
Loop Horace, pedlar, h 59 Gray
Loop Horace W, h foot of High
Loop John, lab, h 8 Washington
Loop Stephen Van Rensselaer, lab, h Baldwin
Loop Timothy, bds 54 Sullivan
Loup Stephen B, blacksmith, h Fifth
LORING J H & CO, (James H L, Edward W Hersey) wholesale grocers, 166 and 168 Water
Loring James H, (J H L & Co) h 272 Water
LORMORE WM J, grocer, 25 Lake, h same
Losey Amos, h cor John and Sullivan

Losey Rutherford M, bds cor John and Sullivan
Losie John, tinner, h 26 DeWitt
Losie Sinclair H, tinner, h 22 Orchard
Losie Thomas M, tinner, h 90 Church
Loughhead John A, moulder, h 34 Hudson
Loughhead William H, moulder, h 25 Hudson
Lovell Harrison T, engineer, bds 82 Baldwin
Lovell Japhet B, teamster, h 82 Baldwin
Lovell John W, tinner, h 8 High
Lowe Miss Caroline F, boarding house, 12 Main
Lowe Uriah S, lawyer, h 14 Main
Lowman H, iron worker, Rolling Mill
Lown Wm, shoemaker, h Fulton nr Broadway
Luce Charles H, N Y Vol, h 69 Gray
Luce Stephen S, clerk, h 7 Gray
Lung Louis, butcher, h 11 Hudson
Lutes Ralsey, N Y Vol, h 371 Water
Lynch Edward, clerk, bds 73 John
Lynch Eli, lab, h 43 First
Lynch Henry, carp, h 32 Water
Lynch John, quarryman, h 73 John
Lynch John. (Mahony & L) h 35 Fourth
Lynch Patrick J, architect, h 17 Magee
Lynch Patrick, teamster, bds 73 John
Lynch Robert, lab, h 85 Second
Lynch Robert, lab, h cor Main and Water
Lynch Sanford, iron worker, Rolling Mill
Lyon John E, clerk, bds 18 Conongue
Lyon Reuben, marble dealer, 60 Lake, h 88 Church
Lyons Miss Harriet, tailoress, h 13 Henry

M

McAsey Patrick J, shoemaker, bds Church
McBride James, shoemaker, Bigelow & Richardson
McCabe Hugh, clerk, bds 30 S Water
McCabe Thomas, clerk, bds 30 S Water
McCafferty John, cigar maker, J I Nicks
McCaffrey Peter, shoemaker, h Hudson, bet Walnut and Hine
McCaffrey Thomas, candle maker, h 114 Lake
McCann James, carp, h 51 Hoffman
McCann Rinaldo, cigar maker, bds 31 Orchard
McCann William, deputy sheriff, h 10 William
McCarty Charles, lab, h cor S Water and Fulton
McCarty Daniel, moulder, h cor Hudson and Walnut
McCarty Daniel, cigar maker, bds cor Hudson and Walnut
McCarty Dennis, lab, h Carroll bet Lake and Fox
McCarty Eugene, cigar maker, h High
McCarty James, lab, h 21 Magee
McCarty James, h Washington av
McCarty John, lab, h 48 Magee

McCarty John, N Y Vol, h 41 Canal
McCarty John, lab, h 19 Jay
McCarty Mrs Mary, h 15 Carroll
McCARTY MICHAEL, marble dealer, 58 Lake, bds Carroll
McCarty Owen, cigar maker, h 66 E Second
McCarty Patrick, lab, h Wisner nr Fifth
McCarty Patrick, lab, h Walnut nr Hudson
McConnell Henry, lab, h 197 Water
McConnell Patrick, lab, h Harriet bet John and Cross
McCoy Alexander, carp, h 107 Lake
McCoy James, lab, h 23 Henry
McCoy Thomas, Eagle Hotel, 85 Wisner
McCoy Wallace, (col'd) lab, h 95 Cross
McDonald Charles, lab, h 205 Wisner
McDonald Stephen, (McD & Palmer) h 26 First
McDonald & Palmer, (Stephen McD, Edward H P) boots and shoes, 115 Water, and tanners, S Lake nr the bridge
McDuffy Charles, painter, bds 31 Conongue
McElroy William H, railroad conductor, h 8 E Second
McGrath George, bds Haight's Hotel
McGraw Patrick, porter, Haight's Hotel
McGREEVY OWEN, livery, cor Lake and Cross, h 21 DeWitt
McInerney Michael, blacksmith, h 20 Washington
McINTIRE HAMDEN W, Johnson's Shingle Machine Manuf, 12 Wisner, bds 27 Conongue
McKee Thomas W, carriage manuf, 63 Water, h 3 Conongue
McKeeby Dyer S, carp, h 82 Main
McKeeby Emly, carp, h 2 Wyckoff's Block
McKibbin Henry, milkman, h 3 Mt Zoar
McKinney Jesse, (McK & Swan) h 22 Jay
McKinney Mathew J, carp, h 12 Orchard
McKinney Mrs Sarah L, h 31 Orchard
McKinney & Swan, (Jesse McK, Robert S) ins agts, 2 Lake
McLaughlin Benjamin, sailmaker, h 87 Church
McLaughlin Mrs Henrietta, tailoress, h 120 Baldwin
McLaughlin John K, moulder, h 9 Dickinson
McLaughlin Silas H, moulder, h 28 E Second
McLean John, lab, h 6 Hatch
McLean Michael, lab, h 6 Hatch
McLean William, Capt U S A, bds American Hotel
McMahon Dennis, lab, h 22 Hatch
McMahon Jeremiah, grocer. 21 Oak, bds Haight's Hotel
McMahon Michael, lab. h 24 Hatch
McMillan Henry, h First av nr S Water
McMillen Mrs Maria. h 17 Jay
McNally Thomas, lab, h cor Franklin and Fulton
McNamee Andrew, tanner, h 8½ Hudson
McNarny Thomas, lab, h cor John and Washington
McNeil Peter S S, spoke manuf, h 23 W Union
McNernan Michael, blacksmith, h 20 Washington
McNerny John, lab, h 93 Lake
McNulty John, lab, h 64 Cross

O. B. NORTHRUP,

Manufacturer of and Dealer in

BOOTS AND SHOES,

No. 152 Water-St.,

ELMIRA, N. Y.,

Three doors west of the Brainard House.

PERSONS desirous of buying GOODS CHEAP FOR CASH will find it to their interest to examine the new and extensive Stock of BOOTS and SHOES of every style and description, just received at No. 152 Water Street, Elmira, N. Y.

The finest SILK GORE HEEL GAITER for $1,00; the best SPRING HEEL GAITER for 50 Cents, and the smoothest MOROCCO SLIPPERS, for four shillings, in Elmira, can be had by calling at Store No. 152 Water Street, three doors west of the Brainard House.

O. B. NORTHRUP.

P. S.—All kinds of work made to order, and Cobbling done in the neatest style.

PRODUCE TAKEN IN EXCHANGE FOR GOODS.

McSolie John, shoemaker, Bigelow & Richardson
McWilliams John A, railroad conductor, h 56 Magee
Macacy Thomas, shoemaker, bds Church
Macacy William, shoemaker, bds Church
Machol Lewis, shoemaker, Haight's Hotel, bds 56 Water
Mack Martin, lab, h 37 Fourth
Mack Michael, lab, h 16 Henry
Mack Mrs Roxana, h 56 Lake
Mack Thomas, lab, h 2 Spring
Macomber Barney, lab, h cor Elm and S Lake
Magill John, (col'd) lab, h 9 Fifth
Mahony James, lab, h 20 Hatch
Mahony Michael, lab, h Hine nr Mt Zoar
Mahony Patrick, lab, h Walnut nr Hudson
Mahony Thomas, (M & Lynch) h 28 Magee
Mahony & Lynch, (Thomas M, John L) grocers, 109 Wisner
Malay William, lab, bds 1 Magee
Mallory Russel, pedlar, h 36 Fourth
Malone John, bds 77 Water
Malone Joseph, carrier *Advertiser*, h 77 Water
Maloney Mrs Hannah, laundress, h First nr Chemung Canal
Maloney John, lab, h 9 Oak
Malson Samuel, (col'd) barber, bds 34 Dickinson
Mapledoram David H, printer, h 8 Columbia
Mander Adam, brewer, Tuthill av foot of Church, h same
Manderville James, boatman, h 85 Second
Mandeville John, baggage man, h 33 Fourth
Maney Andrew, lab, h 59 Factory
Mann Mrs M A, dressmaker, 121 Water, h same
Mannix Maurice, lab, h 21 Third
Mansion House, James Kniskern propr, cor Second and Wisner
Marony John, iron worker, bds 29 Church
Marony Michael, lab, h 42 Fourth
Marony Patrick, lab, h John bet Washington and Orchard
Marony Thomas, iron worker, Rolling Mill
Marsh Aaron T, clerk, h 15 William
Marsh Michael, painter, h 92 Fifth
MARSH WASHINGTON, painter, 5 & 6 Union Block, 168 & 170 Water, h 31 Conongue
Martin John, shoemaker, Bigelow & Richardson
Martin John, lab, at 144 Church
Martin John, ostler, bds 21 DeWitt
Martin Josiah, shoemaker, h cor Harriet and Cross
Mason Mrs Elizabeth, h 290 Water
Mason Marcus, brakeman, h 73 College av
Maston John F, h 26 S Lake
Mathews George, (col'd) lab, h 22 Dickinson
Mathews Mrs Isabella R, h 58 Washington
Mathews Kelsey B, clerk, bds 5 Gray
Mauterstock John, pedlar, h 4 Dickinson
Mauterstock Wm, cooper, h, 4 Dickinson
Maxwell Mrs Catharine, h 8 DeWitt

HORSES AND CARRIAGES

TO LET,

— BY —

O. McGREEVY,

Corner Lake and Cross Sts.,

Opposite Haight's Hotel,

ELMIRA, N. Y.

HOUSES AND LOTS

FOR RENT AND SALE.

Maxwell Edward, lab, h 16 College av
Maxwell Samuel, piano maker, h 28 Washington
Maxwell Mrs Sophia, h Horseheads rd ab Canal
MAXWELL THOMAS, lawyer and pension agent, 7 Lake h 9 S Lake
Mayo Warren E, cooper, h 23 E Union
Maynard Wm H, Ex Messenger, bds Brainard House
Mead Francis S, cutter, Baldwin & Reynolds, bds National Hotel
Mead John T, clerk, h 42 College av
Mead John, carp, h 51 Gray
Mead Mrs Lanor, h 18 Orchard
Mead Peter B, cabinet maker, h 36 Sullivan
Meddaugh Andrew, grocer, 105 Baldwin, h same
Meehan Michael, tobacconist, h 51 William
Meisel Henry, physician, 51 Baldwin, h same
Mekol Louis, shoemaker, bds 56 Water
Melix Mrs Catherine, (col'd) h 27 Dickinson
Melix Sampson, (col'd) lab, h 127 Lake
Melville George S, lawyer, 20 Lake, bds Brainard House
Melville Morton, tailor, h 19 Sullivan
Mercur Mahlon C, coal dealer, head of Dickinson, res Towanda Pa
Merriam William A, baggage master, h 67 Main
Merrill Albert, porter, h 3 Magee
Merrill E C & Co, (Edgar C M, H L Merrill) proprs Delavan House opp R R Depot
Merrill Edgar C, (E C M & Co and W Halliday & Co) bds Delavan House
Merrill Rensselaer R, with E C M & Co, Delavan House
MERWIN WAKEMAN, harness maker, 141 Water, h 42 Washington
Metzger Daniel M, carp, h S Water nr Harmon
Metzger Xavier, butcher, h S Lake nr Miller
Miles Nathan, carp, h Water
Millard Carroll A, engineer, h 61 College av
Miller Mrs E O, dress maker, h 252 Water
Miller Franklin (col'd) lab, h 24 Dickinson
Miller George, engineer, h 23 Baldwin
Miller I L, lab, h 31 W Union
Miller Samuel, shoemaker, h 60 S Water
Milliken Joseph H, cooper, h 5 Dickinson
Millius Henry E, grocer, 218 Water, bds 36 Baldwin
Mills Edwin, carp, boards 67 College av
Mills Joseph P, shoemaker, h 20 Fifth
Mills Richard, pattern maker, h 67 College av
Mills Theodore J, printer, h 6 E Second
Mills William H, engineer, bds 67 College av
Minier Abram, constable, h 6 Mt Zoar
Minier Dennis W, lab, bds Sly's Plot
Minier Fleming, clerk freight office, bds Brainard House
Minier Gideon D, carp, h 15 Jay
Minier George, lab, bds Sly's Plot
Minier Solomon, h 31 Washington
Mitchell Jerome, lab, h 13 Washington
Mitchell John, teamster, h 5 Orchard

W. H. HASKELL,

DEALER IN

Staple & Fancy Dry Goods

GLOVES, HOSIERY, YANKEE NOTIONS, &c.

No. 7 Baldwin Street, (Brainard Block,)

Opposite Post Office

ELMIRA, N. Y.

Mitchell William, clerk, bds 48 William
Mitchell Wm W, artist, 114 Water, bds 48 William
Moffat William, car builder, h 3 College av
Monks James, grocer, 4 Fourth, h same
Monks Thomas R, lab, h 116 Baldwin
Monroe Robert, carp, h 7 Grove
Moody Jacob S, lab, bds 6 Washington
Moody Samuel, lab, h 6 Washington
Mooers Miss Carrie, dressmaker, h 54 Washington
Moon Philemon F, lab, h Franklin nr S Main
Moonan Christopher, grocer, cor Seventh and Hatch, h same
Moonan James, boots and shoes, cor Seventh and Hatch, h same
Moore John H, h Horseheads rd ab Canal
Moore Michael, lab, h Franklin nr S Main
Moore Timothy, lab, h cor Magee and Sixth
Morey Delos C, barkeeper, Elmira Hotel
Morgan Charles, boatman, bds 123 Baldwin
Morgan Peter, boat builder, h 123 Baldwin
Morgan William L, Capt 107 N Y Vol, h 29 S Water
Morgan William L jr, Lieut 107th N Y Vol, bds 29 S Water
Moriarty Mrs Eliza, h 17 Oak
Morrell Alfred L, clerk, bds 63 Baldwin
Morrell Andrew J, barkeeper, bds Franklin House
Morrell C Edward, clerk, bds 42 Baldwin
Morris John, lab, h 73 Main
Morris John, warper, bds 24 Oak
MORRIS RICHARD, grocer, 5 Lake, bds 70 Sullivan
Morrow Flavius W, h 73 Church
Morse Barnet, physician, bds 66 Clinton
Morse Joseph, O, pedlar, h 25 Columbia
Morse Rosius, physician, h 66 Clinton
Moshier Frederick C, clerk, h 72 Second
Moshier Humphrey J, (Bidwell & M) bds 13 W Second
Mott Bernard H, clerk, h 25 Baldwin
MOULTON WM J, photographer and stock dealer, 116 and 118 Water, h 48 William
Mowry Mrs T G, dressmaker, 154 Water, h same
Moyer Lewis H, boatman, bds 125 Baldwin
Moyer Robert E, boatman, bds 125 Baldwin
Mullens Thomas, shoemaker, bds 206 Water
Muller William T, law student, bds 54 Sullivan
Multy John, lab, h Hatch nr Fifth
Munger Harvey J, carp, h foot of High
Munson Edward, carp, h 16 Columbia
Munson Joseph, h 18 First
Murdoch Mrs Elizabeth, h 10 E Union
Murdoch John, lawyer, 101 Water, h 18 College av
Murdock John, (col'd) lab, h 21 Dickinson
Murdock L N, sash maker, h 75 Main
Murgatroyd John, shoemaker, h 17 Orchard
Murphy Anderson, (col'd) lab, h 102 Baldwin
Murphy Mrs Cynthia, boarding house, 93 Cross

Murphy James, lab, h 34 Sullivan
Murphy John C, cooper, bds 7 Ann
Murphy Michael, lab, at Mrs S Maxwell's
Murphy Owen, lab, h 100 Main
Murphy Patrick, lab, h 32 First
Murphy Peter, shoemaker, h 200 Water
Murphy William E, clerk, h Sly's Plot
Murray Alexander, h 7 Mt Zoar
Murray Alexander Jr, carp, h Fulton bet Mt Zoar and Franklin
Murray John, iron worker, h 115 Lake
Murray Maurice, lab, h 30 Hatch
Murray Theron L, machinist, bds 7 Mt Zoar
Murray Timothy, shoemaker, h 64 E Second
Murray Walter, lab, h 196 Church
Musgrave Mrs Agnes M, h 42 Gray
Myers George, furniture finisher, h 92 Church
Myers George W, car builder, h 57 Columbia
Myers Mrs Sarah, h 10 Perry
Myers Willett W, painter, h 28 Cross

N

Naefe Augustus F, painter, h 51 William
Naefe William, painter, h 65 First
Nagle Patrick, lab, h cor Sixth and Magee
Nalon James, lab, h 12 Hatch
Nalon William, iron worker, Rolling Mill
National Hotel, Horatio J Lombard propr, 24 Baldwin
Negus ——, bridge builder, bds 1 Magee
Nelson Alexander, (N & French) h Church nr DeWitt
Nelson D Brainard, teacher, h 36 Baldwin
Nelson Miner, axe maker, bds 93 Cross
Nelson & French, (Alexander N, James S F) grocery etc, 124 Water
Newell Eleazer, lab, h 83 Water
Newkirk William, lab, h 36 Water
Newman Henry, lab, bds 44 College av
Newman Joseph, lab, h 44 College av
Newman M, clothing store, 79 Wisner, h same
Newton A Jerome, (F A Frasier & Co) bds 44 Main
Newton George, bridge builder, bds 1 Magee
Newton Squire, h 44 Main
Newton William T, bds 44 Main
Nichols James K, millinery goods, 105 Water, h same
Nichols John, (col'd) lab, h 12 Oak
Nichols Mrs M A, tailoress, 156 Water, h same
Nickerson Eli, pump maker, h 5 Conongue
NICKS JOHN I, tobacconist, and Assessor U S Internal Revenue, 1 Union Block, 160 Water, h 32 Main
Niver Charles, lab, h 11 N Oak
Nixon John, iron worker, Rolling Mill
Nolton Sherman, h First av nr S Water

Noltz Julius, barber, h 7 S tWaer
Norman John G, blacksmith, Fox nr Carroll, h 83 Church
Norman Mrs Mary Ann, h 28 Sullivan
North Norris, tinner, h 30 Gray
North Norris L, clerk, bds 30 Gray
North Mrs Theodore, h 278 Water
Northrup George E, carp, h 42 S Water
Northrup H G, carp, bds 1 Magee
Northrup Nelson H, h 4 S Main
NORTHRUP OVID B, boots and shoes, 152 Water, bds 382 Water
Norton Charles, lab, h 86 Second
Norton Norman R, lab, h 94 Second
Norton Philander, h 213 Church
Noyes Cephas, shoemaker, h College av
Nye George M, h 33 Main
Nyer Jacob, tailor, h 9 E Union

O

O'Brien Christopher, clerk, bds 61 First
O'Brien Edward, lab, h 5 Hatch
O'Brien Humphrey, mason, h S Water bet Fulton and Harmon
O'Brien James, lab, h foot of Church
O'Brien Jeremiah, lab, h Fulton bet Hudson and S Water
O'Brien John, lab, h Buttonwoods
O'Brien John, marble cutter, h 37 Cross
O'Brien John, mason, h S Water bet Fulton and Harmon
O'Brien John, lab, h 3 Hatch
O'Brien Patrick, blacksmith, bds 3 Conongue
O'Brien Thomas, lab, h 94 Baldwin
O'Brien Thomas, cartman, h 61 First
O'Connell William, shoemaker, h cor Main and Water
O'Connor Daniel, lab, h Elm nr S Main
O'Connor Michael, iron worker, Rolling Mill
O'Day Cornelius, lab, h Sly's Plot
O'Day Mrs Mary, h 20 Henry
O'Day Michael, lab, h 23 Jay
O'Day Michael, lab, bds 20 Washington
O'Dea Andrew, clerk, bds 25 Lake
O'Donnell Bryan, shoemaker, Wilson & Fancher
O'Donnell Charles, lab, h 129 Lake
O'Donnell James, lab, h Clinton Lane, nr E Third
O'Donnell John, boots and shoes, 61 Wisner, h Lake cor Franklin
O'Donnell Mathew, lab, h head of Baldwin
O'Donnell William, shoemaker, at 61 Wisner
O'Driscoll Michael, bds 115 Lake
O'Farrell Michael, lab, h 198 Church
O'Flaherty John, lab, bds 91 College av
O'Flaherty Michael, chair maker, bds Franklin House
O'Keiffe, Cornelius, lab, h 27 Magee
O'Leary Daniel, shoemaker, Bigelow & Richardson

O'Leary Daniel, mason, h 34 Sullivan
O'Maher James, Williamsport and Elmira Hotel, 80 Wisner
O'Niel William, lab, h 23 Magee
O'Regan John, lab, h 69 Fifth
O'Regan John jr, fireman, bds 69 College av
O'Sullivan M, saloon, 16 Wisner, h same
Oakley Oscar R, clerk, bds 28 Baldwin
Odell Isaac, mason, h 76 Fifth
Odell James, N Y Vol, h 8 Hatch
Odell William, lab, h 76 Fifth
Ogden Wm, druggist, 116 Water, h 90 Lake
Oliver Edward, constable, h 12 High
Olivier Louis, teacher, h 207 Church
Olivey William, tailor, h 7 Washington
Olmstead Samuel S, cabinet maker, bds 86 Cross
Oltz Miss Anna, h 85 Water
Orcutt Daniel F, painter, bds 31 Conongue
Osborn Owen N, miller, bds foot of Water
Osborne Hezekiah R, dealer in pianos and melodeons, **h 44 William**
Osborne William H, music teacher, bds 44 William
Overacker Albert W, boatman, h 27 High
Owens Joseph, spinner, bds 63 Factory
Owens Richard, weaver, h 63 Factory

P

Pagett John, leather dealer, bds 206 Water
Pagett William, tanner, 52 Factory, h same
Paine Albert (col'd) lab, h 365 Water
Paine James H, editor, h 8 Main
Palmer Allan, grocer, 10 W Third, h 75 Second
Palmer Edward H (McDonald & P) h 8 S Lake
Palmer George W, carp, h 74 Gray
Palmer J Randolph, bar keeper, Bevier House
Palmer Martin W, blacksmith, 46 Lake, h 89 Gray
Palmenter Nathaniel C, shoemaker, bds Baldwin
Pangburn Henry, lab, h Franklin nr Fulton
Park Henry, tailor, bds Wisner
Parker John, lab, h 90 Second
Parkinson Alexander C, rail road track master, bds **Mansion House**
Parmenter Edward L, h 58 Cross
Parmenter Mrs Martha, bds 226 Water
Parris R, bridge builder, bds 1 Magee
Parsons Granville D, ex messenger, h 8 Orchard
Parsons George W, ex messenger, h 102 Lake
Parsons Miss Sarah E, physician, 28 Lake, bds 24 Carroll
Parsons Theodore S, painter, h 46 Cross
Parsons Wm E, artist, bds 72 Water
Partridge Henry M (Hatch & P) h 71 Lake
Partridge Samuel, h 72 Lake
Patchin Miss Hannah, h Horseheads rd ab Canal

Patchin John, carp, h 54 Fifth
Patten Edward, tanner, bds 112 Baldwin
Patterson James L, cooper, bds 55 William
PATTINSON THOMAS S, meat market, 123 Water, h **34 Baldwin**
Pautz Augustus, grocer, 29 Jay, h same
Pautz Carl, grocer, 33 Fifth, h 109 Baldwin
Paulman Charles, printer, bds Water opp Franklin House
Paulman John, confectioner, h Water opp Franklin House
Paxon James W, iron worker, Rolling Mill
Paxton Joseph, iron worker, h 7 W Union
Pearsall James, carp, at 18 Wisner
Pease Salmon D, farmer, h Hoffman cor Gray
Pechner Mrs Emma, clothing, 153 Water, h same
Pechner Isdell, cutter, h 153 Water
Peck J Franklin, h 40 Main
Peck John A, gunsmith, h 7 S Lake
Pelham Henry, carp, h 274 Water
Pelton Aaron, ex messenger, bds American Hotel
Penoyer James, machinist, at 181 Church
Pennell Mrs Mary, h 57 First
Percival Thomas, lab, h cor Jay and Sullivan
Perine Mrs Clarissa, h S Lake nr Franklin
Perkin Richard, saloon, h 77 Wisner
Perry Commodore (col'd) lab, at 9 S Lake
Perry John K, druggist, 118 Water, h 70 Water
Perry Theodore B, clerk, bds 70 Water
Perry Thomas, (P & Scott, and Carpenter, P & Co) bds Brainard House
PERRY & SCOTT (Thos P, Edwin A S) ins agts, 103 Water over Cook & Covell
Peters H W, mason, h 232 Church
Peterson Edmund, carp, h 68 First
Pettengill John T, engineer, h Beach nr Factory
Pettingale Milton, fireman, bds 54 Second
Pettit Charles P, clerk, bds 118 Cross
Pew Benjamin (col'd) lab, h 28 Fourth
Phelps Frank, lightning rods, h 296 Water
Phillips Miss Helen M, teacher, bds 63 Baldwin
Phillips William H, lumberman, bds Haight's Hotel
Pickering Daniel F, postmaster, cor Baldwin and Carroll, h 38 Baldwin
Pickering Edmund B, carp, bds 55 Cross
Pickering John Jr, clerk, postoffice, bds 55 Cross
Pickering John C, (P & Terry) h 55 Cross
Pickering & Terry, (John P, John K T) carpenters and builders, 24 Main
Pierce Andrew J, clerk, bds 117 Lake
Pierce Azariel B, produce, 97 Water, h 19 College av
Pierce Henry M, clerk, bds 72 Water
Pierce William, clerk, bds 19 College av
Pierce Peter, h 89 Church
Pierson Cyrus, blacksmith, h 111 Church
Pierson Mrs Sarah M, dressmaker, h 4 E Union

Pillbro John, lab, h 33 Fourth
Pinter Joseph, pedlar, h 24 Perry
Pitcher Henry F, carriage painter, bds 14 Jay
Pitts Samuel, engineer, h 10 Oak
Plato M R, lab, h 10 Main
Platt Edward J, express messenger, bds 43 Main
Platt LeGrand, lab, h 245 Water
Plum Hiram A, carp, h First, nr Elm
Plumsted Mrs Sallie M, tailoress, h 40 Sullivan
Poole Michael, lab, h 49 Washington
Poole Patrick, lab, h 16 E Second
Poor Martin, lab, h 46 Wisner
Pope Joseph, bds 5 Conongue
Poppino Richard, h 5 Conongue
Porter Charles H, carp, h 19 Third
Porter D, fireman, bds 1 Magee
Post David, h 40 S Water
POST GARRY H, Union Coffee Mills, 155 Water, bds Brainard House
Post Jacob N, lab, h 236 Church
Post Laskey S, railroad conductor, h 52 Fifth
Post Wm T, County Treas, 159 Water, h Wellsburg rd, Southport
Potter Aaron F, lumberman, h 88 Lake
Potter Cranston T, livery stable, Carroll bet Lake and Baldwin, h 33 William
Potter Mrs Elizabeth, h 24 Carroll
Potter Henry W, machinist, bds 24 Carroll
Powell Charles, barber, bds Elmira Hotel
Powell John, mason, h 1 Orchard
Powell John, lab, h 38 Fourth
Powell Thomas, iron worker, h 40 Fourth
Prall Elon G, carp, bds 64 Gray
Prall J H R, carp, h 64 Gray
Pratt Benjamin H, dentist, bds 72 Water
Pratt Daniel, Elmira Woolen Manufg Co, h 93 Lake
Pratt Daniel R, bookkeeper, Elmira Woolen Manufy, h 8 E Union
Pratt Ransom, Elmira Woolen Manufg Co, h 28 William
Pratt Timothy S, (Rice, Durland & P) h 77 Baldwin
Prescott Joseph S, wines and liquors, 5 Baldwin, bds Haight's Hotel
Prescott William H, clerk, h 5 DeWitt
Preswick Christopher, (P & Dudley) h 6 S Main
Preswick Edmund T, umbrella maker, bds 56 Washington
PRESWICK & DUDLEY, (Christopher P, James T D) booksellers, etc, 114 Water
Price John P, (col'd) barber, 188 Water, h same
Price V R, axe finisher, bds 93 Cross
Priest Charles, bookbinder, h Franklin, nr Fulton
Pross John M, harness maker, bds National Hotel
Pross Joseph, lab, h 31 College av
Pross Samuel, iron worker, Rolling Mill
Pultz ——, tinner, h 5 North Oak
Purcell John, livery, Carroll, nr Lake, h 25 DeWitt
Purcell Patrick, clerk, h 353 Water

Purdy George W, Monitor saloon, 143 Water, h same
Purdy Henry H, physician and surgeon, 31 Baldwin, h 33 Baldwin
Purtell Robert, cartman, h 92 Gray
Purtil Thos, bus driver, Brainard House
Putney Jedediah M, engineer, h 16 First

Q

Qualey James, lab, h 65 Wisner
Qualey Patrick, iron worker, Rolling Mill
Quick Septer P, agt, hats and caps, 135 Water, h S Main cor Henry
Quigley Thomas, lab, h 22 Perry
Quinn John, iron worker, bds 115 Lake
Quinn Simon, lab, bds 74 Church

R

Ragan Timothy, lab, h 14 Canal
Raible Gotleib, lab, h 17 Gregg
Ramsdell Frederick D, ass't postmaster, and grocer, 27 Lake, h 3 Jay
Randall Isaac J, cooper, h Southport Corners
Randall John, machinist, h 60 Baldwin
Randall Merchant, engineer, h 24 Fourth
Ransom Henry, bds 331 Water
Ransom Rastus S, law student, with S C Reynolds, h 29 S Water
Ransom Reuben H, lawyer and justice, 155 Water, h 331 Water
Rapelye Mrs Caroline, h 284 Water
Rapelye Charles A, clerk, post office, bds 284 Water
Rarick Jacob, lab, h 40 Sullivan
Rathbone Miss Catharine E, h 51 Columbia
Rathbone Henry W, Sec'ry and Treas Elmira Rolling Mill Co, h 28 First
Rathbun John, mason, bds 27 Conongue
Rathbun John T, 130 Water, h 94 Lake
Rathbun John Z, physician, bds 108 Lake
Rathbun Peter, clerk, bds 8 S Water
RATHBUN'S BRAINARD HOUSE, Christopher Slater, propr, cor Water and Baldwin
Read Silas, h 269 Church
Read V B, com mer, Basin, h 319 Water
Ready John, ostler, Brainard House
Ready Patrick, clerk, h 61 Gray
Ready Patrick, lab, h 61 Gray
Reall John, lab, h 63 Columbia
Redfield Jared A, general agent E & W R R, h 34 W Union
Redfield John C, barkeeper, bds Franklin House
Redfield Martin A, E & W R R paymaster, h 24 Conongue
Redfield Mrs Matilda, h Henry bet Fulton and Harmon
Reed Charles B, carp, h 19 Hudson
Reed Charles M, engineer, h 15 Gray

Reed Elbridge G, clerk, h 59 First
Reed Henry A, clerk, bds American Hotel
Reed John, clerk, bds 72 Sullivan
Reed John, (col'd) lab, h 22 Dickinson
Reed Judson R, N Y Vol, h 76 Gray
Reeder David, (col'd) lab, at 47 Baldwin
Reeder William T, propr Haight's Hotel, cor Cross and Lake
Rees John W, carp, h 23 Washington
Rees William H, tinner, bds 23 Washington
Reese William, iron worker, h 135 Lake
Reeve Mrs Fanny, boarding House, 63 Baldwin
Reidy John, waiter, Brainard House
Reilly Edmund, baker, h 283 Church
Reilly Henry, lab, at 33 Baldwin
Reimer Carl, lab, h 109 Baldwin
Renshaw George, machinist, h 62 Second
Reynolds Absalom G, grocer, h 68 Main
Reynolds Adna H, agt, h 61 Baldwin
Reynolds D D & Co, (David D R, Albert S Saterlee) grocers, 21 Lake
Reynolds David D, (D D R & Co) h 39 Baldwin
Reynolds David S, edge tool maker, h 10 DeWitt
Reynolds George G, clerk, bds 30 William
Reynolds Isaac, h 6 S Water
REYNOLDS JOHN A, physician, 41 Baldwin, h same
Reynolds John A, bds 80 Lake
Reynolds Mrs Lydia T, h 104 Lake
Reynolds Mrs Mary J, (col'd) h 17 Jay
Reynolds Nathan, h 80 Lake
Reynolds Samuel N, (Baldwin & R) h 243 Church
Reynolds Samuel T, h 104 Lake
Reynolds Schuyler C, lawyer, 137 Water, h 5 Gray
Reynolds Stephen, (col'd) lab, h 131 Lake
Reynolds William, bowling saloon, cor Wisner and Third, h 17 East Union
Rhoades Harvey O, wagon maker, at 3 Carroll
Rhoades Isaac, carp, bds Jay
Rhoades Peter, (Cook, Willis, Bedell & Co) h 72 Fifth
Rhoades William, lab, h 78 Walnut
Rice Aaron, physician, 32 S Lake, h same
Rice Albert L, clerk, bds 32 S Water
Rice Daniel O, grocer 182 Church, h 188 Church
RICE, DURLAND & PRATT, (Remick C R, Daniel T D, Timothy S P) dry goods, 122 Water
Rice Edmund, painter, h 94 Fifth
Rice Gustavus, (E Lehman & Co) 151 Water
Rice Henry S, lawyer, bds 32 S Water
Rice Leman, artist, bds 32 S Water
Rice Remick C, (R, Durland & Pratt) h 25 William
Rice Samuel, tel operator, bds American Hotel
Richards Richard, lab, h 7 Columbia
Richardson Charles W, (col'd) lab, h 56 Lake
Richardson Jackson, (Bigelow & R) bds Brainard House

Richardson John, shoemaker, h Buttonwoods
Richardson Daniel, shoemaker, h Southport
Richardson Lewis S, railroad conductor, bds American Hotel
RICHARDSON MICHAEL, dry goods, 170 Water, h 29 Conongue
Richardt George H, barber, Brainard House, h 14 Jay
Rider Lewis, shoemaker, A L Derby
Rider William, pedlar, bds 208 Water
Ridley Barzilla, carp, h 38 W Union
Riggle John, lab, h 63 Washington av
Riggs Rev Joseph L. h 320 Water
Riker John W, painter, h S Lake
Riker Samuel, h 46 Baldwin
Riker Samuel jr, printer, bds 46 Baldwin
Riley John, carp, h cor S Water and Harmon
Riley Mrs Martin, h 34 Carroll
Riley Timothy, shoemaker, h Walnut nr Hudson
Ripley P B, Pedlar, h 44 Gray
Ritz Adam, lab, h 19 Jay
Roach James, lab, Haight's Hotel
Roach John F, lab, h 7 Dickinson
Robbins Benjamin V, clerk, bds 38 Washington
Robbins Joseph, taxidermist, bds 6 S Lake
Robbins Miss Mary A, music teacher, bds 32 Baldwin
Roberts Charles V, blacksmith, bds 3 Orchard
Roberts Edward P, iron worker, h 6 Perry
Roberts Ezra M, teacher, h 50 William
Roberts Henry S, blacksmith, h 3 Orchard
Roberts James, moulder, h 29 Orchard
Roberts Thomas, barkeeper, bds 20 Orchard
Roberts William, dyer, 69 Water, h same
Robertshaw John, cook, Brainard House
Robertson Archibald, (Smith, R & Fassett) h Fulton bet Elm and Mt Zoar
Robertson James, gilder, bds National Hotel
Robinson George M, clerk, bds 6 William
Robinson John, butcher, bds 208 Water
Robinson John M, furniture manuf, cor Church and William, warerooms 43 Lake, h 6 William
Robinson Newel R, butcher, h 92 Lake
Robinson Noah H, (R & Ingraham) h 92 Lake
Robinson Richard W, clerk, bds 92 Lake
Robinson William H, clerk, bds 6 William
Robinson & Ingraham (Noah H R, Clark S I) druggists, 24 Lake
Robjohn William, organ builder, h 17 Gray
Rockwell Orville, h 45 First
Rockwell Silas B, h 33 Orchard
Roe Edward D, farmer, h 183 College av
Roe John C, h 35 Main
Roe W Fletcher, teacher, h 179 College av
Rogers George (col'd) lab, h 30 Dickinson
Rogers George W, N Y Vol, h 247 Church
Rogers J Henry, meat market, 6 Lake and 214 Water, h 8 Ann

Rogers John, lab, h 15 First
Rogers John, ostler, bds 32 Baldwin
Rogers Joseph, rail road conductor, bds 1 Magee
Rogers Orlando, carriage maker, h 38 Water
Rogers Peter, stone cutter, h Fulton bet Hudson and S Water
Rogers Patrick, lab, h Canal bank bet Church and First
Rogers Stephen, stone mason, h Canal bank bet Church and First
Rohan Martin, lab, h S Lake nr Mt Zoar
Romer Anthony (Bower & R) bds American Hotel
Roody James F, bds 102 Church
Roof John J, ex messenger, h 347 Water
Roonan Patrick, lab, h 16 Water
Roosa Augustus P (G W Scardefield & Co) h 324 Water
Rose Enoch L, axe maker, h 38 Orchard
Rose Stephen jr, clerk, bds 63 Baldwin
Rosebrook Emory W, contractor, h 48 Second
Rosenbaum Leman (Guttenburg R & Co) res Montrose Pa
Rosenblat Levi, priest jewish synagogue, h 10 High
Rosenthall Moses, pedlar, h cor John and High
Ross Abner C, shoemaker, h 3 Ann
Ross Alfred D, clerk, bds 3 Ann
Ross Joshua C, brick maker, h 30 Jay
Rothwell Edwin, cooper, John Wormley
Roulet William, jeweler, bds 84 Lake
Rourke Mrs Mary, h 6 DeWitt
Rowland ——— bridge builder, bds 1 Magee
Rowland Chas H, clerk, bds 118 Cross
Rowley Nimrod, (col'd) mason, h Hudson nr Western limits
Rozell George H, lab, h 3 Ann
Rubens David R, clothier, 145 Water
Ruff John, cabinet maker, h 30 Water
Rumsey Mrs Caroline D, h 33 Hudson
Rumsey Charles E, ex messenger, bds Brainard House
Russell David, lab, h Sly's Plot
Russell John, iron worker, h 100 Baldwin
Russell John R, lab, bds Sly's Plot
Russell Orrin, carp, bds 127 Lake
Russell Peter R, mason, bds National Hotel
Russell W C, shoemaker, h Water
Rutter James H, station agent Erie railway, h 52 William
Rutter William E, car maker, h 11 Third
Ryan Edward, lab, h 62 Second
Ryan Edward, lab, h cor Fifth and Wisner
Ryan James, iron worker, h 191 Wisner
Ryan John, lab, bds 62 Second
Ryan John, lab, h Davis nr Sixth
Ryan John D, carp, h 32 E Second
Ryan Joseph, lab, h First nr Wisner
Ryan Timothy, lab, bds 62 Second

S

St Peter and Paul Church, (catholic) cor High and Cross, Rev Martin Kavanagh, pastor
Sackett Caleb W, h 39 Water
Sackett John H, carp, h 86 Church
Sackett Richard, pump manuf, 61 Water, h 42 Water
Saddler Timothy, with T S Pattinson, h 5 Ann
Sampson Joseph C, (W W Ballard & Co) bds Brainard House
Samuels Albert (L Straus & Co) bds Haight's Hotel
Samuels David, foreman Rolling Mill, bds 117 Wisner
Samuels David W, iron worker, h 33 Conongue
Sanders Wayland M, music teacher, h 103 Lake
Sarford John, (col'd) lab, h 30 Conongue
Sarsfield Michael, shoemaker, h 28 Water
Satterlee Albert S, (D D Reynolds & Co) bds 17 E Union
Satterlee Elias B, (Tuthill Brooks & Co) h 6 Gray
Saunders Alfred, h 56 Factory
Saunders Grover, carp, at 12 Wisner
Saunders Lucius J, mason, h 20 Henry
Savey Stephen, farmer, h S Main nr Franklin
Savey Stephen, lab, h Mt Zoar nr Southern limits
Sayles Henry, physician, (and Kelly, Biggs & Co) 35 Baldwin, h same
Sayles Henry, dentist, bds 35 Baldwin
Scales Nathaniel, shoemaker, bds ——
Scanlon Simon, iron worker, h 23 Canal
SCARDEFIELD G W & Co (George W S, Augustus P Roosa) gilders, looking glass and picture frame manuf, 11 Baldwin
Scardefield George W (G W S & Co) 11 Baldwin
Schabel Robert, butcher, h 8 N Oak
Scharf Edward, butcher, h Jay
Schleicher William, saloon, 23 Baldwin, h same
Schlosser J Jacob, blacksmith, h 26 E Second
Schlutter Ernst, piano varnisher, h 19 Wisner
Schoenemann Louis, tailor, h 23 Baldwin
Schuszler George F, mason, bds 10 Mt Zoar
Scofield Lewis D, h 44 Wisner
Scott Edwin A (Perry & S) h 53 Fourth
Scott Mrs Jane, h 10 Washington
Scott William M, bds 49 Baldwin
Scutt Alvah M, carp, h 23 Sullivan
Scutt Merritt L, carp, h 9 Mt Zoar
Scutt William, bds 23 Sullivan
Searles John E, carp, h 7 Hudson
Sears Mrs Mary, tailoress, h 42 Cross
Sears William, h cor Oak and Washington av
Sebaskey M, clothing store, 75 Wisner, h same
Sechler Charles, iron worker, bds 11 Magee
Second Presbyterian Church, cor Church and Lake, Rev Isaac Clark pastor
Secor David R, tobacconist, h 52 High
See James L, piano maker, h 85 Church

20 and 22 Lake Street, Elmira, N. Y.

STUART & UFFORD,

MERCHANT TAILORS,

Manufacturers of and Dealers in every variety of

𝔐𝔢𝔫'𝔰 𝔒𝔩𝔬𝔱𝔥𝔦𝔫𝔤 𝔞𝔫𝔡 𝔉𝔲𝔯𝔫𝔦𝔰𝔥𝔦𝔫𝔤 𝔊𝔬𝔬𝔡𝔰.

HATS,	TRUNKS,	CANES,
CAPS,	VALISES,	FURS,
BOOTS,	SACHELS,	ROBES,
SHOES.	UMBRELLAS.	&c., &c.

Also, the largest assortment of

LADIES' FURS

in Southern New York.

PARTICULAR ATTENTION GIVEN TO THE

MILITARY AND CUSTOM DEPARTMENTS.

Cheapness and *Superiority* are the watchwords of our well-known firm, and *One Price and No Deviation* its time-honored motto.

STUART & UFFORD,
20 AND 22 LAKE-ST.

Seely Absalom, soda water manuf. 18 S Lake, h same
Seeley Lewis B, shoemaker, h 83 Water
Seely Wm T, artist, cor Lake and Carrol, h 75 Columbia
Sellinger John, butcher, bds 93 Water
Selover John, planing mill, 42 Fifth, h 101 College av
Selway James B, cooper, h 4 Magee
Seward Hector M, h 80 Cross
Shaddock Luke, carp, h 55 First
Shaft Alpheus D, lab, h 38 Magee
Shaft E D, iron worker, Rolling Mill, h Magee
Shannon Cyrus, lab, h 2 Wykcoft's Block
Shannon Martin, machinist, at 181 Church
Shanon Patrick, lab, h 201 Wisner
Shaver Charles, iron worker, bds 46 Cross
Sharfe Edward, butcher, h 1 E Third
Sharp John, lab, h 1 Canal
Shattuck Charles S W, shoemaker, h 5 W Union
Shaw George, pedlar, bds 208 Water
Shaw H L, h 286 Water
Shaw Samuel, painter, h 112 Baldwin
Shay Michael, lab, bds 25 Water
Shay Phillip, lab, h 32 First
Shay Robert, moulder, bds 19 Henry
Shay Timothy, lab, h 25 Water
Shearman John jr, millinery goods, 137 Water, h same
Sheehain Peter, sawyer, h 225 Wisner
Sheehan Dennis, lab, h 72 Washington av
Sheehy John, clerk, h 6 Orchard
Sheive George, h 16 S Main
Sheive John L, clerk, bds 173 Water
Shephard John, (col'd) lab, h 8 Dickinson
Shephard Michael, cooper, h 57 Baldwin
Shepherd Wm R, clerk, bds cor W Union and Fourth
Sherman Eli B, mason, 228 Church
Sherman George, telegraph operator, bds 226 Church
Sherwood Joseph L, ship carp, h 51 Dickinson
Shew Mrs Edith, glove maker, h DeWitt nr E Second
Shiedlen & Bush, (Ernst S,———B) furniture manuf, 183 Water
Shields John, mason, h 14 Oak
Shives John M, butcher, bds Elmira Hotel
Shockey George W, clerk, bds 6 Washington
Shockey Lewis R, ostler, bds Water
Shoemaker James M, barkeeper, Arbour Hotel
Shorts Jeremiah, (col'd) lab, h 26 Conongue
Shuart David, carp, bds 4 Magee
Sickles Daniel, carp, h 104 Baldwin
Sigison William, cooper, 87 Baldwin, h 83 Lake
Simonds Daniel, laborer, h 17 Washington
Simons Charles, (S & Co) h 40 Carroll
Simons Charles jr, (S & Co), h 40 Carroll
SIMONS & CO, (Charles Simons, Charles Simons, jr,) **confectioners and umbrella makers, 40 Carroll**

Simons Josiah C, (Hutchins & Co) h 24 Third
Simmons Robert, cloth presser, bds 72 Sullivan
Sittinfild Solomon, pedlar, bds 43 Cross
Sivalls Charles, National Garden and Saloon, Carroll bet Lake and Baldwin, h same
Skehan James, lab. h First nr Wisner
Skidmore George H, express messenger, h 5 College av
Skindle Richard, (col'd) carp, h 35 Dickinson
SLATER CHRISTOPHER, propr Brainard House, cor Water and Baldwin
Sloan Thomas, lab, h 18 Hatch
Sly John H, h cor Elm and S Lake
Sly Mathew M, h cor Ann and Sly
Sly William K, clerk, National Hotel
Smith ——, bridge builder, bds 1 Magee
Smith Alonzo D, bookkeeper, h 351 Water
Smith Benjamin A, tailor, h 75 Sullivan
Smith Calvin L, (col'd) barber, bds 95 Cross
Smith Charles A, jeweler, bds 84 Lake
Smith Charles B. cutter shoe dep't Stuart & Ufford, h 5 College av
Smith Daniel G, carp, h 58 William
Smith David D, (col'd) lab, h 118 Baldwin
Smith Ecker, (col'd) lab, h Fulton bet Hudson and Henry
SMITH ELIJAH B, baker and confectioner, 1 Brainard Block, bds 54 William
Smith Elkany, cooper, h 266 Water
Smith Frank, carp, h 62 Main
Smith Gabriel L, (S & Spaulding) h 60 Sullivan
Smith George, (col'd) lab, bds 21 Dickinson
Smith H B, Sup't Susq Div E R'y, h 74 College av
Smith H Boardman, (S, Robertson & Fassett) h 270 Church
SMITH HARVEY, grocer, 131 Water, h 8 S Main
Smith Harvey H, boarding house, 28 Baldwin
Smith Henry, (col'd) lab, h 17 Dickinson
Smith Hiram F, tailor, h 22 S Lake
Smith Hudson, clerk, bds 74 Second
Smith Huron O, carp, 18 Wisner, h Harmon nr Henry
Smith Isaac S, carp, h 15 Hudson
Smith Rev James H, h 113 Baldwin
Smith John, cartman, h 1 Washington
Smith John, (col'd) lab, h 16 Dickinson
Smith John R, machinist, bds Bevier House
Smith John S, propr Franklin House, 230 Water
Smith Lewis M, (Ward & S) bds 74 Second
Smith Lucius M, carp, h 46 Fourth
Smith Michael, lab, h John nr Canal
Smith Norman, physician, bds 79 John
Smith Oliver D, grocer, cor Fifth and Wisner, h same
Smith Orlando N, clerk, h 79 John
Smith Robert E, carp, h 25 Gray
Smith, Robertson & Fassett, (H Boardman S, Archibald R, Newton P F) lawyers, 1 and 2 Ely Hall

Smith Robert T, machinist, h 194 Lake
Smith Rodney B. h 56 William
Smith Seymour, Sup't bridge repairs. E & W R R, h 62 College av
Smith Solomon P, cooper, h 270 Water
Smith Thomas J, (col'd) clothes cleaner, h 39 Dickinson
Smith Timothy J, clerk, bds National Hotel
Smith Uriah, physician, h 25 College av
Smith William, (cold'd) lab, h 2 Fourth
Smith William A, shoemaker, bds 51 Cross
Smith William B, h 74 Second
Smith William C, clerk, bds 29 Conongue
Smith William S, carriage maker, 46 Lake, h 9 High
Smith & Spaulding (Gabriel L S, Thomas S S) lawyers, 149 Water
Smoke Benjamin W, tailor, h 82 Church
Smyth George, lab, h 63 High
Snell Chauncey, blacksmith, h 82 Second
Snowden George W, (col'd) lab, bds 124 Baldwin
Snowden Philip, (col'd) lab, h 124 Baldwin
Snowden Samuel, (col'd) lab, h Fifth
Snyder George W, (Herrick & S) h Southport
Snyder H S, carp, h Washington av
Snyder Henry, iron worker, bds Gandam's saloon
Snyder Jacob, saloon, 137 Wisner, h same
Snyder Lewis, barkeeper, Western Hotel
Soper Royal R, law student, bds 12 Main
Soper Samuel, boatman, h 77 Columbia
Soule Charles H, merchant, bds 54 Fifth
Spaulding Charles H, clerk, h 31 Main
Spaulding George, baker, bds Chemung House
Spaulding Henry C, lumber and coal dealer, h 31 Main
Spaulding Isaac P, brakeman, h cor Fourth and Dickinson
Spaulding Thomas S, (Smith & S) h 21 Broadway
Spencer Edward, carp, h 364 Water
Spencer William H, shoemaker, at 61 Wisner
Sperry Medad, cooper, bds 38 W Union
Spickerman Levi, carp, bds 74 Gray
Spies Mrs Charlotte, tailoress, h 10 N Oak
Spilland John, shoemaker, Bigelow & Richardson
Splen William, lab, h Hudson bet Harmon and Fulton
Spraggett Richard, Third Ward Hotel, 6 S Lake
Squire Truman H, physician, 136 Church, h same
Squires Montgomery N, cigar maker, h 44 Fourth
Stagg William E, bookkeeper, h 85 Lake
Stanchfield John K, physician, 47 Baldwin, h same
Stancliff Lewis J, Pres Elmira Bank, h 13 Clinton
Stanford Edward A, barber, bds 19 Lake
Starks William H, railroad conductor, h 15 College av
Steele Frederick C, grocer, 15 and 17 Lake, h 31 S Water
Steele Mrs Theodore, boarding house, 66 Main
Steeples John, hatter, h 104 Church
Stepfield Daniel S, h Horseheads rd ab Canal
Stephens Daniel, h 68 Lake

G. W. WATERS,

Portrait & Landscape Painter,

No. 135 Water Street, Elmira, N. Y.

All kinds of Photographs Colored in a superior manner. Fine Landscapes and Figure Pieces on sale. Instruction given in the various branches of Oil Painting, Dawing in Pencil, Crayon, Sketching from Nature, Perspective, &c.

MICHAEL McCARTY,

MARBLE CUTTER,

AND DEALER IN

MANTLES, MONUMENTS & HEAD STONES,

No. 58 Lake Street, Elmira, N. Y.

FARMERS & CITIZENS

DINING SALOON,

173 Water-St.

CHARLES HAMILTON, Proprietor.

Warm Meals at all Hours.

Stephens John, bds 68 Lake
Stephens Robert, law student, bds 68 Lake
Sterling William A, lab. at 73 Church
Stern Moses, (D Straus & Co) res Wellsville
Stevens Charles, shoemaker, Bigelow & Richardson
Stevens Lafayette, machinist, h 72 Gray
Stevens Mrs Mary, h 79 Church
Stevens Samuel, miller, h 70 Gray
Stewart Charles, h 4 Ann
Stewart Robert A, machinist, bds National Hotel
Stewart Thomas H, (col'd) lab, h 86 Baldwin
Stewart William, boatman, h 200 Church
Stiles Isaac, shoemaker, 35 Lake, h 56 Cross
Stiles Isaac P, shoemaker, bds 56 Cross
Stiles Samuel, printer, bds 56 Cross
Stilson William, shoemaker, h 109 Lake
Stockweather George, boatbuilder, bds with H S Snyder
Stocum Mrs C M, milliner, 134 Water, up stairs, h same
Stocum Eliphalet, carp, Cross nr Lake, h 134 Water
Stoddard Holmes, lab, h 7 W Union
Stoll Joseph C, saloon, 101 Wisner, h same
Stoll William, h 264 Church
Stoll Wm H, clerk, bds 264 Church
Stone David J, carp, h Mt Zoar, nr Southern limits
Stone Err, carp, h Fulton nr Mt Zoar
Stone Henry S, clothier, h Franklin nr S Main
Stone Lorain J, carp, h Broadway nr Mt Zoar
Stone Newton A, carp, h 274 Church
Story Charles F, carp, h 49 Baldwin
Stow Charles W, lab, h 16 DeWitt
Stowell A, carp, h 7 Willow
Stowell Abel, carp, h 21 William
Stowell Charles M, carp, bds 21 William
Stowell Francis A, clerk, bds 21 William
Stowell John E, clerk, bds 21 William
Stowell Mrs Sarah, dressmaker, h 12 College av
Stowell William H, clerk, bds 21 William
Strachen John, blacksmith, h 4 Dickinson
Strachen Thomas, blacksmith, 88 Baldwin, h Dickinson
Straight William E, orderly sergt, U S disbursing office
Strang Henry W, clerk, bds 74 Lake
Strang Samuel B, h 74 Lake
Stratton John C, lab, h 27 Sullivan
Straus D & Co, (David S, Moses Stern) mer tailors, 139 Water
Straus David, (D S & Co) h 56 Water
Straus Henry D, clerk, bds 56 Water
Straus L & Co, (Louis S, Geo Hochstetter, Albert Samuels) dry goods, 164 Water
Straus Louis, (L S & Co) bds Brainard House
Strawn A B, mason, bds Mansion House
Strong Dennis (col'd) lab, h 16 Perry
Struthers Robert, iron worker, h 37 Dickinson

Stryker Samuel G, mer tailor, 10 Lake, h 6 Ann
Stryker Seth C, clerk, bds 6 Ann
Stuart ——, bridge builder, bds 1 Magee
Stuart Charles B, (S & Ufford) h 132 Church
STUART & UFFORD, (Charles B S, Daniel E U) mer tailors, boots and shoes, hats, caps and furs, etc, 20 and 22 Lake
Stuempfle John, blacksmith, h 45 Dickinson
Suffern Miss Eliza, h 24 High
Sullivan Bartholomew, lab, h Broadway nr Fulton
Sullivan Cornelius, lab, h 98 Main
Sullivan Cornelius, foreman Mercur's coal yard, h nr head Dickinson
Sullivan Daniel, lab, h Walnut nr Hudson
Sullivan Mrs Deborah, h cor First and Chemung Canal
Sullivan J Michael, printer, bds 8 Fox
Sullivan John, blacksmith, h 50 College av
Sullivan John, lab, bds cor First and Chemung Canal
Sullivan John, lab, h 73 Sullivan
Sullivan John, lab, h S Water bet Fulton and Harmon
Sullivan Patrick, lab, bds 209 Wisner
Sullivan Patrick, lab, h River bank nr Hudson
Sullivan Thomas, lab, h River bank, nr Fulton
Sullivan William, carriage maker, h 8 Fox
Surgenty Joseph, tailor, h 13 Gregg
Susbery Samuel, (col'd) boatman, bds 13 Dickinson
Susbery Willis, (col'd) boatman, h 13 Dickinson
Sutton Nelson, spinner, h 66 Factory
Swails Mrs Joanna, h 25 Jay
Swails Stephen A, boatman, h 25 Jay
Swan Robert, (McKinney & S) h 30 S Water
Swansbrough Leonard, lab, h 88 Gray
Swartz Fabian, h 43 Cross
Swayze Wilson S, mason, h 6 Jay
Sweeney John, lab, cor High and E Third
Sweet Asa W, carp, h 28 S Lake
Sweet Wesley, chair maker, h 31 William
Sykes Jesse F, harness maker, h 15 Orchard
Sykes Warren F, bds 15 Orchard

T

Tackman Frederick, cabinet maker, h 13 Orchard
Tanner Mrs Elizabeth, h 8 Jay
Tate John, h 11 Henry
Taylor Abraham J, tanner, h 57 Factory
Taylor Benjamin W, boatman, h 40 Carroll
Taylor Mrs Charity (col'd) laundress, h 14 Perry
Taylor Elias W, ointment maker, h 78 Fifth
Taylor Odell, carp, bds 57 Factory
Taylor Richard, (col'd) lab, h 6 Dickinson
Taylor Samuel B, jeweler, bds 93 Cross
Taylor Silas B, boat builder, bds Canal Junction

Taylor Silas G, clerk, h Canal Junction
Temple Mrs N C, h 65 Gray
Tenbroeck Peter B, wagon maker, h 40 Washington
Tenbroeck William R, clerk, bds 40 Washington
TENNY DeWITT C, physician, (and T & Co) 200 Water, house 42 William
Tenny & Co, (DeWitt C T, Nathan B Evans) druggists, 200 Water
Terry Ebenezer, drayman, bds 206 Church
Terry John K, (Pickering & T) h 10 Hudson
Terwilliger John L, carp, h 62 Cross
Thayer Wm M, (T & Whitley) bds 63 Baldwin
THAYER & WHITLEY, (William M T, John W Jr) eds and proprs ELMIRA DAILY PRESS cor Lake and Water
Third Ward Hotel, Richard Spragget propr, 6 S Lake
Thomas Henry, (col'd) lab, h 106 Baldwin
Thomas James M, saddlery hardware, (and T & Barnes) bds 7 Gray
Thomas John, (col'd) lab, h 28 Conongue
Thomas John G, machinist, bds Troy House
Thomas Joseph, lab, h 115 Lake
Thomas Samuel, (col'd) lab, h 30 Perry
Thomas Thomas M, iron worker, h 90 Baldwin
Thomas William, (col'd) whitewasher, h 14 Dickinson
Thomas & Barnes, (James M T, Wm H B,) silver platers 38 Carroll
Thompson Albert H, shoemaker, h cor S Main and Henry
Thompson George, clerk, bds American Hotel
Thompson Mrs H I, millinery rooms, 129 Water, bds Brainard House
Thompson Isaac S, shoemaker, bds cor S Main and Henry
Thompson J Russell, lumberman, h cor Lake and Washington av
Thompson James, lab, h cor Fourth and Davis
Thompson Jeremiah, cartman, h 14 First
Thompson John T, painter, h 6 Grove
Thompson John M, butcher, h Hatch nr Fifth
Thompson William, cartman, bds 14 First
Thompson William C, h 30 S Lake
Thornton William, (col'd) lab, h 41 Dickinson
Thorp John, lab, h 113 Second
Thro C & J, (Charles and Joseph) Western Hotel, 141 Wisner
Thro Charles, (C & J T, Western Hotel
Thro David C, ex messenger, h 117 Lake
Thro Joseph F, (C & J T) h 116 Lake
Thurber Benjamin H, clerk, bds Haight's Hotel
Thurber Mrs Hannah A, boarding house, 30 Baldwin
Thurston Ariel S, lawyer, 15 Lake, h 87 Lake
Thurston Miss C, teacher, h 41 Main
Tidd Horton, editor ELMIRA GAZETTE, bds Haight's Hotel
Tierney Daniel, lab, h 22 First
Tierney Daniel, lab, h 5 Hatch
Tierney Michael, barkeeper, Brainard House
TILLMAN JOHN M, harness maker, 41 Lake, h 40 High
Tillson James, machinist, h 113 Lake
Tilly Alexander, brewer, h 60 Second
Tilly Arthur T, carp, bds 60 Second

Timms Wm, pedlar, h 111 Gray
Todtmann Mrs Julia, grocery, 87 Church, h same
Toles Mrs Sarah M, h 21 E Union
Tomlinson, Solomon B, lawyer and county clerk, h 76 W Second
Tompkins Solomon, painter, h 12 Hudson
Tompkins William C, harness maker, h 88 Gray
Town Hall, Cross bet Lake and Baldwin
Towner James A, news agt, post office building, h 134 Church
Tongue Jonathan, carp, h 48 Main
Toole John, clerk, bds Wmspt & Elmira Hotel
Tracy William, Fireman, bds 1 Magee
Trainor James, lab, h 39 Canal
Trainor James, lab, h 10 Canal
Trainor John, lab, bds 10 Canal
Trapp Wm, h 29 W Union
Traver Miss Betsey, h 44 Clinton
Traver Solomon, lab, h 23 Baldwin
Traver William, teamster, h 84 Baldwin
Treadwell Hezekiah D, (Gilbert & Co) h 340 Water
Trescott Elisha, clerk, bds 49 William
Trescott J W, harness maker, h 10 William
Trevor Mrs Anna C, h 156 Church
Tripp Alfred, lab, bds 206 Water
Tripp Edward, machinist, bds Troy House
Troppit Henry, lab, h Oak nr Fifth
Trout Miles, blacksmith, bds 3 Conongue
Troy House, N R Updike propr, 105 Wisner
Truesdell Warren, clerk, bds 118 Cross
Tupper Wm H, pedlar, h 1 Walnut
Turner David, (col'd) lab, h Franklin nr S Main
Turner Robert T, law student, bds 63 Baldwin
Turner Thomas H (col'd) lab, h 49 Dickinson
Turner William, shoemaker, h Elm nr S Main
Turner Wm jr, shoemaker, bds Elm nr S Main
TUTHILL, BROOKS & CO. (David H T, Henry S B, Elias B Saterlee) dry goods and groceries, 132 Water
Tuthill David H, (T, Brooks & Co) h 65 Lake
Tuttle Eliada, collector and carrier *Elmira Press*, bds 28 Baldwin
Tuttle Wilbur F, law student, bds 5 Gray
Tyler Asher, Prest Elmira Rolling Mill Co, h 13 Main
Tyler Richard H, umbrella maker, h 24 Fourth

U

Ufford Daniel E (Stuart & U) bds Haight's Hotel
UNION COFFEE MILLS, G H Post propr, 155 Water
United States Ex Co, Sutherland DeWitt agt, 16 Baldwin
Up DeGraff Samuel F, shoemaker, h 2 Hudson
UPDEGRAFF THAD S, Oculist and Aurist, 151 Water, h 80 Clinton
Updegraff Edon, carp, h cor Broadway and Main

Updegraff Elbridge, painter, bds 31 Conongue
Updegraff Jacob, machinist, h 80 Gray
Updike Nelson R, Troy House 105 Wisner

Vail Benjamin, cabinet maker, h 26 Gray
Vail Charles M, carp, h 36 College av
VanAllen Daniel, h 3 Columbia
VAN CAMPEN SAMUEL R, banker, corner Water and Baldwin, (Brainard Block) bds 92 Cross
VanDoren William, bds 43 Main
VanDusen Francis C, clerk, bds Haight's Hotel
VanKirk James L, (V & Knapp) h Church bet Columbia and Davis
VanKirk & Knapp, (James L V, Annanias K) meat market 220 Water
VanLew George, flour and feed, h 1 Gray
VanNorman Samuel, butcher, h 38 First
VanOver George, engineer, h 48 Fourth
VanPelt Aaron, shoemaker, h 10 Mt Zoar
VanTassel Daniel, law student, bds 12 Main
VanTassel Richard W, machinist, h 34 Fourth
VanWagoner Cornelius, teamster, bds 94 Fifth
VanWagoner Henry, teamster, h 94 Fifth
Vanderbilt William, tanner, h 10 Henry
Vandyne James A, carp, h 34 E Second
Vanseay Jason, pedlar, h 7 Hudson
Vaughn Harmon P, cooper, h First av, nr S Water
Vaughn Willard, cooper, h Water
Vermilya Edgar D, engineer, bds 4 E Union
Vermilya Mrs Hannah S, dressmaker, h 4 E Union
Vermilya John L, tinner, h 2 Columbia
Vernooy Epenetus, wagon maker, h 12 Gregg
Vernooy Miss Margaret C, dressmaker, bds 21 E Union
Vernooy Samuel, carp, h 68 William
Vernooy Wessel, teamster, h 43 Clinton
Vescelius W Irving, prof of penmanship, 18 Lake, bds 17 William
Viall Ethan, street com, bds 94 Church
Viall William, lumber dealer, cor Church and Chemung Canal, h 46 Gray
Vickery Samuel, lab, h 37 DeWitt
Vincent Gillett J, clerk, bds Haight's Hotel
Vincent Joseph, lab, h 8 Hatch
Vinton Charles E, (V & Chamberlin) bds 37 Wisner
Vinton & Chamberlin, (Charles E V, John W C) wines and liquors, 25 Wisner

Wade Joseph, lab, h foot of High
Wagemann Albert, variety goods, 121 Water, h same

Wagener Peter, porter, Haight's Hotel, h 12 Washington
Wager Peter, grocer, bds 230 Church
Wagner John S, barber, 206 Water, h same
Wales Ira, shoemaker, bds 254 Water
Walker Alonzo P, carp, h 81 Church
Walker George, tailor, 8 Lake, h Hudson nr Hind
Walker Henry, carp, bds 81 Church
Walker James, plumber, h Hudson nr Western limits
Walker Thomas, iron worker, Rolling Mill, h Willow
Wallace Richard K, painter, 60 Lake, h 34 William
Wallace William, saloon, 93 Wisner, h same
Waltner Michael, brewer, h 51 William
Walters George A, brakeman, bds 19 Sixth
Walters Orin, lab, h 230 Church
Walters Orin C, propr Bevier House, 117 Wisner
Walters R E, railroad conductor, h 19 Sixth
Walters William, machinist, bds Troy House
Watzer Peter N, saloon, 93 Water, h same
Ward Amos, lab, h 88 Gray
Ward J Ralph, (W & Smith) bds 92 Cross
Ward Moses, car builder, h 81 Church
Ward William, lab, h 59 Gray
Ward & Smith, (J Ralph W, Lewis M S) lawyers, 135 **Water**
Warn Cornelius, fireman, h 13 Magee
Warner Eli, clerk, bds 17 College av
Washington Henry, (col'd) barber, bds 34 Dickinson
Washington Hiram, (col'd) lab, h 26 Fifth
Washington James, (col'd) lab, h 30 Perry
Washington John, (col'd) lab, h 25 Dickinson
Wass Joseph, iron worker, bds Gandam's saloon
WATERS GEORGE W, portrait painter, 135 Water, h 2 Gray
Watkins James, (col'd) lab, h Franklin nr S Main
Watley Henry, lab, h 4 Mt Zoar
WATROUS RIGGS, hardware, etc, 112 Water, h 53 Lake
Watson William H, (col'd) lab, h 121 Lake
Watts John, h 1 S Water
Watts Robert M, foreman *Press*, bds 1 S Water
Watts Stephen, lab, h 2 Dickinson
Watts William, lab, h 114 Lake
Waugh John, h 71 Second
Way Charles, tavern, 89 Baldwin
Weaver Jesse, lab, h 67 Wisner
Webner John, shoe maker, bds Mansion House
Webster Daniel, tobacconist, J I Nicks
Webster Daniel, (col'd) lab, h John bet Washington and Orchard
Wedge Luther, engineer, h 24 Third
Weed Peter, clerk, bds 35 DeWitt
Weed Phineas, clerk, bds 35 DeWitt
Weed William B, lab, h 35 DeWitt
Weibel Joseph, saloon, 143 Wisner, h same
Weir William C, h 1 Orchard
Welch A, carp, h cor Factory and Beach

Welch Alexander, grocer, 13 Baldwin, h 231 Church
Welch Charles, hackman, bds 231 Church
Welch James, fireman, bds 1 Magee
Welch James, h 61 Columbia
Welch James, lab, h 28 Hatch
Welch John, engineer, h Davis nr Fourth
Welch Michael, lab, h Lock No 2 Junction Canal
Welch Morris, lab, h Fulton, bet Hudson and S Water
Welch Warner H, propr Elmira Hotel, 182 Water
Weldner George, shoemaker, 77 Water, h same
Weller Miss Electa, clerk, bds 3 Washington
Wellington Isaac M, principal Elmira Academy, h 32 Fourth
Wells Chauncey E, druggist, 156 Water, h 340 Water
Wells John C, h 234 Church
Wells Nelson, boots and shoes, 29 Lake, h 43 Gray
Welton Michael, carp, h 14 Cross
Werner Maurice, clothier, 111 Water, h 26 High
West C F & Co, (Charles F W, and ——) millers, Water nr Newtown Creek
West Charles F, (C F W & Co) h foot of Water
West Thomas D, tanner, h 195 Water
Westlake Henry D, clerk, bds Haight's Hotel
Wey William C, physician and surgeon, 68 Water, h same
Weyer Philip, grocer, 29 E Union, h same
Wheeler Eli, h 45 William
Wheeler Leverett R, h 5 S Water
Wheeler Orrin H, bag maker, h 241 Church
Wheeler R F, h 1 Walnut
Wheeler Willie, physician, bds Bevier House
Whipple Albert R, h 8 Hudson
White Calvin S, shoemaker, h 94 Church
White Charles, iron worker, Rolling Mill
White Charles E, printer, bds 35 Hudson
White Daniel M, clerk, bds 72 Water
White George, railroad conductor, bds American Hotel
White Jonathan M, shoemaker, bds 254 Water
White Patrick, lab, h 26 Hatch
White Spencer H, shoemaker, h 54 Washington
White William, tanner, h 76 High
White William L, painter, bds National Hotel
Whiting Seth T, carriage maker, 201 Water, h 40 Baldwin
Whitley John H, artist, h 14 High
Whitley John Jr, (Thayer & W) bds 28 Baldwin
Whitney Mrs Anna, h 21 Jay
Whitney Samuel, shoemaker, h 2 Wyckoff's Block
Whiton George L, N Y Vol, h 226 Water
Wicks John, lab, bds 19 College av
Wiegarty Henry, carp, bds 42 High
Wilcox Mrs Anna R, h 114 Baldwin
Wilcox Howard M, clerk, bds 15 William
Wilcox Isaac, bds National Hotel
Wilcox James, bds National Hotel

GRIDLEY & DAVENPORT,

DEALERS IN

HARDWARE AND NAILS,

COOKING & PARLOR STOVES,

Hot-Air Furnaces, Registers, Ventilators, &c.

—ALSO—

PAINTS & OILS,

and Manufacturers of

TIN, COPPER & SHEET-IRON WARE,

No. 109 Water Street, Elmira, N. Y.

G. A. GRIDLEY.   E. DAVENPORT.

Wilcox Thomas, lab, h cor Fulton and Hudson
Wilken Moses B, railroad conductor, h 15 Columbia
Wilkey James A, shoemaker, h Southport
Wilkinson M C, Capt 107 N Y Vol, h 24 W Union
Williams Arthur T, printer, h 4 Gray
Williams Dever, clerk, bds 18 Conongue
Williams E J, clerk Express Co, h 276 Water
Williams Edward H, cabinet maker, h 44 Cross
WILLIAMS ERASTUS, grocer, 19 Lake, bds 15 William
Williams Evan, iron worker, h 123 Lake
Williams George, pedlar, bds 208 Water
Williams Henry, (col'd) lab, h 115 Baldwin
Williams James W, tanner, h 69 Gray
Williams John D, canal collector Junction Canal, cor Conongue and Clinton, h 46 William
Williams John, (col'd) lab, h 24 Conongue
Williams John P, machinist, h 4 College av
Williams Mrs Mary, h 5 Jay
Williams Richard P, printer, bds Church nr Canal
Williams S Quincy, clerk, bds 18 Conongue
Williams Samuel, axe maker, bds 93 Cross
Williams Samuel, (col'd) lab, h 30 Dickinson
Williams Mrs Sophia (col'd) h 86 Baldwin
Williams Thomas B, brakeman, bds Troy House
Williamsport & Elmira Hotel, James O'Maher, propr, 8 Wisner
Willor Frederick, carp, h 200 Water
Wilson Charles F, (W & Fancher) h 288 Water
Wilson Henry, clerk, bds 6 Gray
Wilson James, lab, h 105 Second
Wilson Jonas D, ag't J I Nicks, bds 32 Main
Wilson Wm R, Capt N Y Vol, h 72 Second
Wilson & Fancher, (Charles F W, Sutherland F) boots and shoes, 104 Water
Wind Thomas Jr, iron worker, Rolling Mill
Wise Ambrose, tobacconist, h 32 DeWitt
Wise Charles, bridge builder, bds 1 Magee
Wise Daniel, bridge builder, bds 1 Magee
Wisner Jeffrey A, railroad conductor, h 57 Sullivan
Wisner Mrs Mary, h 12 S Main
Wisner Mrs Mary A, h 54 Sullivan
Wisner Wm H, clerk, bds Brainard House
Wisner Wm H, saloon, 28 Lake, h 96 Church
Wiswell Miss Clara I, dressmaker, bds 46 Cross
Wittenberg Mrs Rosa S, h 44 Baldwin
Wixon Silas, teamster, h 28 Orchard
Wolcott Mrs Charlotte, h Broadway nr Mt Zoar
Wolcott George A, lab, h Franklin nr Fulton
Wood Andrew J, engineer, h 72 Sullivan
Wood Annanias (col'd) lab, h Franklin nr Fulton
Wood Calvin, carp, h 88 Gray
Wood Coe, lab, h Factory
Wood Frank, carp, h 58 Columbia

Wood John A, lab, bds 72 Sullivan
Wood John B, (col'd) lab, h 18 Dickinson
Wood Joseph, carp, bds 50 High
Wood Seymour B, tinner, h 25 S Water
Wood William, machinist, h 335 Water
Wood William H, carriage maker, h 76 Church
Woodcock Edward, lab, Water Cure
Woodruff Albert, carp, h 84 Gray
Woods James L, (Hathaway & W) h 304 Water
Woodward William, lumberman, h 73 Baldwin
Wormley John, cooper, foot Sly, h 9 Ann
Worrall George, grocer and coal dealer, 66 William, h 49 William
Wright Mrs Eliza, dressmaker, h 12 College av
Wright George B, railroad conductor, h 55 Fourth
Wright John S, lab, h 54 Gray
Wright Thomas S, hatter, h 55 Fourth
Wright William, bds 48 Main
Wyckoff Arcalus, (W & Bro) h 8 S Water
Wyckoff Charles W, (W & Bro) h 24 Hudson
Wyckoff Charles W Jr, carp, 12 Wisner, bds 24 Hudson
Wyckoff Elias, carp, h S Water, nr Harmon
Wyckoff & Bro, (Arcalus, and Charles W) manufs water-pipes, etc. 12 Wisner
Wynn Hugh, iron worker, h 41 Canal
Wynn James, lab, h 10 Hatch
Wynn John, iron worker, h 23 Canal
Wynn Thomas, iron worker, h 10 Hatch

Y

Yates Wm, jeweler, bds 228 Water
YATES WM P, Watches and Jewelry, 147 Water, h 228 Water
Yeoman Milton, carp, h 56 S Water
Young C, engineer, bds 1 Magee
Young David, clerk, h 24 DeWitt
Young Jesse, tailor, Baldwin & Reynolds, h Southport
Young Michael, shoemaker, h 69 Water
Young Peter C, h 44 Washington
Young Thomas, match manuf, Horseheads rd ab Canal, h same

BUSINESS DIRECTORY.

Agents—Insurance.

AYRES SOCRATES, 99 Water
McKinney & Swan, 2 Lake
PERRY & SCOTT, 103 Water
Robinson Noah H, 24 Lake

Artists—Photograph and Ambrotype.

Doty C C, (3 Union Block,) 164 Water
Hart A P. 22 Lake
Mitchell Wm W, 114 Water
MOULTON W J, 116 and 118 Water
Seeley Wm T, cor Lake and Carroll

Portrait and Landscape Painter.

WATERS G W, 135 Water

Auction and Commission Merchants.

COWEN & SON, 12 Lake

Bakers and Confectioners.

Blampied John 107, Wisner
Blampied Joshua, 196 Water
COKE LEVI, 31 Lake
SMITH E B, 1 Brainard Block

Banks and Bankers.

Bank of Chemung, 130 Water
Chemung Canal Bank, 74 Water
Elmira Bank, 14 Baldwin
Elmira Savings Bank, 151 Church
VAN CAMPEN S R, cor Water and Baldwin, (Brainard Block)

ELMIRA
INSURANCE OFFICE,

No. 101 Water St., Elmira, N. Y.

(OVER COOK & COVELL'S HARDWARE STORE.)

NEW ARRANGEMENT.

THE subscribers would announce to the public that the Insurance business heretofore carried on by LAWRENCE & PERRY and PALMER & SCOTT, is now united in one Office, and that they are authorized to transact any business for Companies formerly represented by the two Offices. They respectfully solicit a continuance of the business of the old customers of the two agencies, as well as a liberal share of new Insurance business.

They represent the following first-class New York and Hartford Companies:

		Capital & Surplus.
ÆTNA,	Hartford,	$2,683,000
CONTINENTAL,	New York City,	1,200,000
SECURITY,	"	648,045
LORILLARD,	"	596,899
MANHATTAN,	"	362,000
METROPOLITAN,	"	383,414
PHŒNIX,	"	298,222
LAMAR,	"	341,205
ATLANTIC,	"	250,000
MARKET,	"	262,000
PHŒNIX,	Hartford,	500,701
MERCHANTS,	"	256,000
NORTH AMERICAN,	"	314,788
CITY FIRE,	"	302,314
THAMES,	Norwich,	127,000

CONNECTICUT MUTUAL LIFE INSURANCE COMPANY, Hartford, Conn., accumulated capital $5,000,000.

N. B.—Drafts on England and Ireland for sale in sums to suit.—Also, Passage Tickets for sale for the Liverpool, New York, and Philadelphia Steamship Company, which line consists of Ten Steamers, mostly all new.

THOMAS PERRY.
EDWIN A. SCOTT.

PERRY & SCOTT, Agents.

Barbers.

Bailey F J, 19 Lake
Hill Charles J, Haight's Hotel
Hoppe Charles, 131 Water
Hunt William C, National Hotel
Price John P, 188 Water
Richardt George H, Brainard House
Wagner John, 206 Water

Billiard Rooms.

ARBOUR, 7, 9 and 11 Lake
Bradley Thomas, Baldwin, opposite Brainard House
DeWitt Charles, 169 Water

Blacksmiths.

Davis Chancellor L, 100 Cross
Higgins Norman L, 3 Carroll
Krowl Abraham, 38 Lake
McKee Thomas W, 63 Water
Norman John G, Fox nr Carroll
Palmer Martin W, 46 Lake
Strachen Thomas 88 Baldwin

Book Binders.

Bookmyer Frederick, 117 Water
FAIRMAN & DEVOE and LOUIS KIES, 2 and 4 Lake

Booksellers and Stationers.

HALL BROTHERS, 128 Water
PRESWICK & DUDLEY, 114 Water

Boots and Shoes—Manufacturers and Dealers.

Berhalter Joseph, 105 Church
Bigelow & Richardson, Water nr Wisner
Blos Francis, 27 E Union
Burbage John, 191 Water
Coulton Edward V Jr, 36 Water
DERBY A L, 154 Water
Gilbert & Co, 125 Water
HUTCHINSON S S, 126 Water
McDonald & Palmer, 115 Water
Machol Lewis, Haight's Hotel
Moonan James, cor Seventh and Hatch
NORTHRUP O B, 152 Water
O'Donnell John, 61 Wisner
Stiles Isaac, 35 Lake

S. AYRES'
INSURANCE AGENCY,

No. 99 Water Street, Elmira, N. Y.

	ASSETS.
HOME INSURANCE COMPANY, of New York City,	$1,521,268
HARTFORD FIRE INSURANCE Co., of Hartford, Conn.,	885,570
NORTH WESTERN INS. Co. of Oswego, N. Y.,	260,502
ARCTIC FIRE INS. Co., New York City,	304,526
SPRINGFIELD FIRE & MARINE INS. Co., Mass.,	412,086
ALBANY CITY FIRE INS. Co., Albany, N. Y.,	107,228

Applications received for Insurance in either of the above Companies, also in other responsible New York Companies. Losses will be equitably adjusted and promptly paid.

S. AYRES,
Watch-Maker and Jeweler,

NO. 99 WATER STREET, ELMIRA, N. Y.,

Keeps a Full Stock of Goods on hand, in his line, such as

Gold & Silver Watches, Silver & Plated Ware,

JEWELRY,

Spectacles, Clocks, Cutlery, &c., &c., &c.

All kinds of work usual in his line done promptly.

STUART & UFFORD 20 and 22 Lake
Wells Nelson, 29 Lake
Wilson & Fancher, 104 Water

Brewers.

Bevier & Briggs, Second nr Wisner
Mander Adam, Tuthill av foot of Church

Butchers.

Baker Sparrow, 194 Water
Bidwell & Moshier, cor Church and Wisner
Brand John, 1 S Lake
Haase Henry, 105 Church
Haunstein Heinrich, 32 Lake
Hitchcock & Loomis, 89 Wisner and 39 Lake
Fahr Peter, 29 E Union
PATTINSON T S, 123 Water
Rogers Jonathan H, 216 Water and 6 Lake
Van Kirk & Knapp, 220 Water

Carriage Manufacturers.

Ewing James, cor Cross and William
Herrick & Snyder, cor Cross and Fox
Smith William S, 46 Lake
Whiting Seth F, 201 Water

Clothing—Manufacturers and Dealers.

Atkins Christopher C, cor Lake and Water
BALDWIN & REYNOLDS, 149 Water
Bower & Romer, 119 Water
CASS JOHN, cor Baldwin and Water
Gladke Joseph, 113 Water
Guttenberg, Rosenbaum & Co, 162 Water
Jacobs J, 127 Water
LEHMAN E & CO, 151 Water
Newman M, 79 Wisner
Pechner Mrs E, 153 Water
Rubens D R, 145 Water
Sebasky M, 75 Wisner
Straus D & Co, 139 Water
Stryker S G, 10 Lake
STUART & UFFORD, 20 and 22 Lake
Walker George, 8 Lake
Werner M, 111 Water

Crockery, China and Glass Ware.

DEXTER & ELMORE, 158 Water
Dunn D T, 2 and 4 Lake

Elmira Mills, Elmira, N. Y.

[LATE ELY'S MILLS.]

SAMUEL HOTCHKIN,

WHOLESALE & RETAIL DEALER IN

Flour, Corn Meal, Feed,

OATS, SHORTS, BRAN,

GRAHAM FLOUR, RYE FLOUR, &C.,

AT THE LOWEST RATES.

ORDERS PROMPTLY FILLED.

Cash Paid for all kinds of Grain.

☞ Goods delivered within the Corporation Free of Charge.

Coal—Dealers in.

Baldwin J D, 112 Cross
Barclay Coal Co, Junction Chemung and Pennsylvania Canals
Haskell & Bro, 14 Gray
Langdon & Co, 46 Fifth
Mercur Mahlon C, head of Dickinson
Worrall George, 66 William

Coffee and Tea.

UNION COFFEE MILLS, G H Post, 155 Water

Dentists.

Armitage William F, 100 Water
Conkey and French, 116 ½ Water
Eaton Lewis, 147 Water
Hines W A, 133 Water

Dry Goods—Dealers in.

Bulmer D, 108 Water
COVELL E & Co, 106 Water
Dormaul Elias H, 134 Water
Dunn D T, 2 and 4 Lake
French Philip, 171 Water
HART WM E, 110 Water
HASKELL WM H, 7 Baldwin
RICHARDSON MICHAEL, 170 Water
RICE, DURLAND & PRATT, 122 Water
Straus L & Co, 164 Water
TUTHILL, BROOKS & CO, 132 (old No 34) Water

Drugs and Medicines—Dealers in.

COVELL JOHN D, 102 Water
Frasier F A & Co, American Hotel
Kellogg & Hevener, 133 Water
Ogden Wm, 116 Water
PERRY JOHN K, 118 Water
Robinson & Ingraham, 24 Lake
Tenney & Co, 200 Water
Wells C E, 156 Water

Dyers.

Beckwith James B, 51 Water
Roberts William, 69 Water

JOHN CASS,

MERCHANT TAILOR,

WHOLESALE AND RETAIL DEALER IN

READY-MADE CLOTHING,

Gents' Furnishing Goods, Hats & Caps.

Corner Water and Baldwin Streets,   ELMIRA, N. Y.

JOHN K. PERRY,

Wholesale and Retail Dealer in

DRUGS & MEDICINES,

CHEMICALS, PERFUMERY,

Window Glass, Paints and Oils, Patent Medicines,

KEROSENE OIL & ALCOHOL, BY THE BARREL,

FANCY ARTICLES, &C.

No. 118 Water St., - - - - Elmira, N. Y.

Edge Tools Manufacturers.

Beardsley Benoni P, 50 Lake

Florist.

Brockmuller John C, cor William and E Third
Humphrey George W, 20 E Second

Flour Manufacturers.

HALLIDAY W & CO, Elmira Steam Mills, Basin
HOTCHKIN SAMUEL, Elmira Mills, Water, near College Avenue
WEST C F, Water, near Newtown Creek

Furniture—Manufacturers and Dealers.

HUBBELL S B, 174 Water
La France P A, Agt, 159 Water
Robinson John M, 43 Lake
Shiedlen & Bush, 183 Water

Gas Fitters.

COOK & COVELL, 101 and 103 Water
DEXTER & ELMORE, 158 Water

Gilders and Picture Frame Manufacturers.

SCARDEFIELD, G W & CO, 11 Baldwin

Glue—Manufacturers.

Carpenter, Perry & Co, Tuthill Avenue, near Church
Eliason, Greener & Co, Factory foot of John, Office 147 Water

Gunsmith.

De Witt Wm P, 83 Water

Groceries and Provisions—Dealers.

Assauer Christian, 273 Union
Barton & Dickinson, 8 Lake
Billette Joseph, 188 Water
Billings John L, 32 Water
Birdsall Oliver, 47 Main
Blampied Joshua, 196 Water
Bolt Martin S, 50 Second
Brand John, 1 S Lake
Bulmer D, 108 Water
Bundy O F & J A, 37 Lake

BURNS THOMAS, 95 Water
Carpenter, R T, 100 Water
COKE LEVI, 31 Lake
Couch Stephen B, Canal Junction
COVELL E & CO, 106 Water
DeWitt A M, 19 Baldwin
Dunn D T, 2 and 4 Lake
Goldsmith Benjamin, 55 Water
Gorman Dennis, 113 Wisner
Haas Henry, 105 Church
HART WM E, 115 Water
Huntley & Cole, 129 Water
Hutchins & Co, 218 Water
Kellogg & Hevener, 133 Water
Kingsbury Wm A, 222 Water
Lee Thomas, (col'd) 51 Wisner
LORING J H & CO, 166 and 168 Water
LORMORE W J, 25 Lake
McMahon Jeremiah, 21 Oak
Mahony & Lynch, 109 Wisner
Millius Henry E, 218 Water
Monks James, 4 Fourth
Moonan Christopher, cor Seventh and Hatch
MORRIS RICHARD, 5 Lake
Nelson & French, 124 Water
Palmer Allan, 10 West Third
Pautz Augustus, 29 Jay
Pautz Carl, 33 Fifth
Ramsdell F D, 27 Lake
Reynolds D D & Co, 21 Lake
Rice Daniel O, 182 Church
Smith Harvey, 131 Water
Steele F C, 15 and 17 S Water
Welch Alexander, 13 Baldwin
Meyer Philip, 29 E Union
WILLIAMS E, 19 Lake
Worrall George, 66 William

Hardware, Stoves and Tin Ware----Manuf's and Dealers.

Armitage Richard F, 214 Water
BROWN WM, 14 and 16 Lake
COOK & COVELL, 101 and 103 Water
GRIDLEY & DAVENPORT, 109 Water
Hamilton Walter, 36 Lake
WATROUS RIGGS, 112 Water

Harness, Saddles and Trunks.

Knapp William B, 75 Water
MERWIN W, 141 Water
TILLMAN JOHN M, 41 Lake

Hats, Caps and Furs—Manufacturers and Dealers.

COMSTOCK S G, 150 Water, 2 Brainard Block
GARDINER, N W, 117 Water
STUART & UFFORD, 20 and 22 Lake
Quick S P, 135 Water

Hotels.

American Hotel, cor Third and Wisner
Bevier House, 117 Wisner
Chemung House, 29 Baldwin
Delavan House, cor Wisner and Clinton
Eagle Hotel, 85 Wisner
Elmira Hotel, 182 Water
Exchange Hotel, 139 Wisner
Franklin House, 230 Water
Haight's Hotel, cor Cross and Lake
Hoffman's Hotel, 157 Wisner
Mansion House, cor Second and Wisner
National Hotel, 24 Baldwin
RATHBUN'S BRAINARD HOUSE, cor Water and Baldwin
Third Ward Hotel, 6 S Lake
Troy House, 105 Wisner
Western Hotel, 146 Wisner
Williamsport and Elmira Hotel, 80 Wisner

Intelligence Office.

BARR GABRIEL, 56 Lake

Iron—Manufacturers & Dealers. (*See also Hardware, &c.*)

Dyer Morgan, cor Water and Wisner
Wheeler Eli, Yard Magee's Basin
Dounce William J, 48 Fifth

Johnson's Patent Shingle Machine Manufactory.

MC'INTIRE HAMDEN W, 12 Wisner

Justices of the Peace.

Davis George L, 105 Water
DeWitt James, 4 Lake
Denton S B, 2 Lake
Ranson R H, 155 Water

Lawyers.

Babcock E F, 160 Water
Beebe George, 4 Lake
Brush George A, 157 Water
Davis George L, 105 Water
DeWitt James, 4 Lake
Diven A S & G M, 153 Water
Gibbs Levi, 105 Water
Hardy James H, 103 Water
Hart E P, 15 Lake
Hathaway & Woods, 151 Water
King Rufus, 137 Water
Kingsley Wm C, with Hathaway & Woods
Maxwell Thomas, 7 Lake
Melville George S, 20 Lake
Murdoch John, 101 Water
Ransom R H, 155 Water
Reynolds & Benn, 20 Lake
Smith, Robertson & Fassett, 1 and 2 Ely Hall
Smith & Spaulding, 149 Water
Thurston A S, 15 Lake
Tomlinson S B, County Clerk's Office
Ward & Smith, 135 Water

Livery.

Cook Thomas, Bevier House
Fassett Truman, Cross, between Lake and Baldwin
McGREEVY OWEN, cor Lake and Cross
POTTER CRANSTON T, Carroll, between Lake and Baldwin
Purcell John, Carroll, near Lake

Marble Dealers.

Baker Nathan, 79 Water
Lyon Reuben, 60 Lake
McCARTY MICHAEL, 58 Lake

Military Goods.

COLLINGWOOD BROTHERS, 13 Lake
STUART & UFFORD, 20 and 22 Lake

Newspapers.

ELMIRA ADVERTISER, (Daily and Weekly,) 8 Lake
ELMIRA GAZETTE, (Daily and Weekly,) 2 and 4 Lake
ELMIRA PRESS, (Daily,) cor Lake and Water.

News Dealers.

Brink Miss Mary A, 120 Water
Towner James A, Postoffice building

Oculist and Aurist.

UP DE GRAFF T S, 151 Water

Painters, Paper Hangers and Glaziers.

Davis Alvin, 164 Church
La France P A, 159 Water
MARSH WASHINGTON, 5 and 6 Union Block, 168 and 170 Water
Wallace Richard K, 60 Lake

Physicians.

Benjamin Henry L, 38 Main
Chubbuck Hollis S, 36 Baldwin
Comfort Eli C, cor Lake and Carroll
Flood Patrick Henry, 44 Water
Gardiner Nicholas D, 4 Lake
Goodman William F. (col'd) 52 Lake
Gray P Wells, (homeo) 8 Ely Hall
Hart E L, 78 Lake
Hart Ira F, 147 Church
Lee Thomas J, 22 Henry
Meisel Henry, 51 Baldwin
Morse Barnet, 66 Clinton
Morse Rosius, 66 Clinton
Purdy Henry H, 31 Baldwin
Reynolds John A, 41 Baldwin
Rice Aaron, 32 S Lake
Sayles Henry, 35 Baldwin
Stanchfield John K, 47 Baldwin
Squire Truman H, 136 Church
Wey William C, 68 Water

Piano Forte Manufacturers and Music Dealers.

ELIASON, GREENER & CO, 160 Church, and 147 Water

Printers—Book and Job.

FAIRMAN & DE VOE, 2, 4, 6 and 8, Lake
THAYER & WHITLEY, Daily Press Office

Restaurants.

ARBOUR, 7 9 and 11 Lake
Baker James M, 190 Water
Bortle Ephraim, 192 Water
Elmendorf & Beers, 23 Lake
HAMILTON CHARLES, 173 Water

Silver Platers

Thomas & Barnes, 38 Carroll

Tanners.

McDonald & Palmer, S Lake near the Bridge
Pagett William, 52 Factory

Tobacco and Cigars—Manufacturers and Dealers.

BARTHOLOMEW U, 9 Baldwin
GILL BROS, 198 Water
LEVY MAURICE, 33 Lake
NICKS JOHN I, (1 Union Block) 160 Water

United States Internal Revenue Stamps Depository.

VAN CAMPEN S R, Brainard Block

Umbrella Manufacturers.

Elmira Umbrella Manufg Co, cor Fourth and Magee

Watches and Jewelry—Manufacturers and Dealers.

AYRES S, 99 Water
Badger L M, 103 Wisner
COLLINGWOOD BROTHERS, 13 Lake
Hamilton Daniel S, 36 Carroll
Johnson Thomas, 22 Carroll
YATES WM P, 147 Water

Wines and Liquors, (Wholesale.)

Dowling Laughlin, 18 Baldwin
Howes Ephraim W, 9 Fox
LORING J H & CO, 166 and 168 Water
Prescott Joseph S, 5 Baldwin

L. COKE,
LAKE ST. BAKERY,
NO. 31 LAKE STREET, ELMIRA, N. Y.

MANUFACTURER OF

BREAD, CRACKERS, PIES & CONFECTIONERY,
PLAIN & ORNAMENTAL CAKES

of the best manufacture. Also, dealer in Fruits, Vegetables, Choice Family Groceries and Refreshments.

N. B.—All orders promptly executed on the most reasonable terms.

ARNOT'S MILLS.

C. F. WEST, PROPRIETOR.

East end of Water St., Elmira, N. Y.

WHOLESALE AND RETAIL DEALER IN

Flour, Grain, Meal, Mill Feed, &c.

CUSTOM GRINDING

Done satisfactorily on short notice.

CAYUGA PLASTER

Always on hand at the lowest market price.

COWEN & SON,

Auction & Commission Merchants,

and Wholesale and Retail Dealers in

YANKEE NOTIONS,

PEDDLERS' GOODS, CROCKERY WARE,

Table and Pocket Cutlery,

BOOTS & SHOES,

Whips, Spool Thread, Hoop Skirts, Dress Goods,

PERFUMERY, &C., &C.

Merchants supplied with many articles at less than New York Prices.

No. 12 Lake Street, Elmira, N. Y.

T. C. COWEN.   T. A. COWEN.

More books from New York History Review

A Short and Sweet History of the Chemung Valley

The Park Church Souvenir Cookbook of 1906

The Great Inter-State Fair

Zim's Foolish History of Elmira

Zim's Foolish History of Horseheads

Frederick Douglass' Speech at Elmira

In Their Honor

In Dairyland

The True Stories series

A Brief History of Chemung County

Cartoons and Caricatures

Our Own Book

The Elmira Prison Camp

www.ingramcontent.com/pod-product-compliance
Lightning Source LLC
Chambersburg PA
CBHW070552160426
43199CB00014B/2467